Political
Rhetoric

Aristole - available
means of persuasion

The Presidential Briefings Series
Robert J. Spitzer, Series Editor

The Presidential Briefings Series provides concise and readable introductions to topics of concern to those who have been and will be President of the United States. By approaching their subjects from the vantage point of what a president most needs to know, and what the citizenry most need to know about the presidency, these books are authoritative and significant works on subjects related to the presidency.

Previously published and forthcoming works include:

Political Rhetoric by Mary E. Stuckey
Making Foreign Policy Decisions by Christopher J. Fettweis
Presidential Leadership in an Age of Change by Michael A. Genovese
Packing the Court by Nancy Maveety

means of persuasion

PRESIDENTIAL BRIEFINGS

Political
Rhetoric

MARY E. STUCKEY

Transaction Publishers

New Brunswick (U.S.A.) and London (U.K.)

Library of Congress Catalog Number: 2014035435
ISBN: 978-1-4128-5681-2 (cloth); 978-1-4128-5613-3 (paper)
eBook: 978-1-4128-5631-7
Printed in the United States of America

Library of Congress Cataloging-in-Publication Data

Stuckey, Mary E.
    Rhetoric : a presidential briefing book / Mary E. Stuckey, Department of Communication.
        pages cm
    Includes bibliographical references.
    ISBN 978-1-4128-5681-2 (cloth) -- ISBN 978-1-4128-5613-3 (pbk.)
1. Presidents--United States. 2. Presidents--United States--Language. 3. Rhetoric--Political aspects--United States. 4. Political oratory--United States. 5. Communication in politics--United States. 6. United States--Politics and government. I. Title.
    JK516.S778 2015
    320.97301'4--dc23

                                                                    2014035435

This book is gratefully dedicated to
Martin J. Medhurst
And
David Zarefsky

CONTENTS

Acknowledgments   ix

Introduction: Communicating the Presidency   xi

1   The Public, the Media, and the Presidency   1

2   Rhetoric from an Institutional Perspective   21

3   Managing Rhetorical Opportunities   43

Conclusion: Presidents and Their Rhetoric   69

Bibliography   81

ACKNOWLEDGMENTS

First, I'd like to thank Tom Langston for asking me to participate in this series. Tom was a valued colleague and he will be much missed. Chris Fettweis, who is continuing Tom's good work, provided valuable advice and made many helpful suggestions. Jennifer Nippins and the team at Transaction Publishers have been wonderful to work with.

The book was drafted while I was on a PROF leave provided by the College of Arts and Sciences at Georgia State University. My thanks to the Dean's office and to my Chair, who conspired to make the leave possible. During that semester, I also spent some time in Washington, DC, at the National Archives and at the Library of Congress. While there, I was a Visiting Scholar at the APSA Centennial Center for Political Science and Public Policy and a Presidency Research Group Fellow. I'm grateful to APSA for its support. That opportunity also allowed me access to the library at George Washington University, and the librarians there were both kind and helpful. I very much appreciated the kindness and scholarly acumen of the archivists at the LOC and the National Archives.

I'm also grateful to those who took time out of their preposterously busy schedules to read and comment on earlier drafts of chapters. John Murphy, Trevor Parry-Giles, and Colleen Shogan deserve special thanks. Jason Edwards, Cara Finnegan, and John Rountree generously helped with citations. And, as usual, all gratitude to David Cheshier, who, in addition to his other talents, is a walking bibliography of all things rhetorical.

My life would sometimes be easier if he had fewer sources at his fingertips, but my work would be much weaker.

I agreed to work on this project while I was teaching a graduate seminar on presidential rhetoric, and that little bit of serendipity worked very much to my advantage. Even more than usual, then, I am grateful to my students, who challenged my thinking, inspired me with their interest, and honored me with their insights. Students in past seminars also helped me think through some of the issues I write about here, so thanks to Sara Baugh, Caleb Cates, Eugenia Ferrero, Zoe Hess Carney, Evan Johnson, Phil Kostka, Stephen Heidt, Rob Mills, Kim Overmier, Reynolds Patterson, and Milene Ortega Ribeiro.

This may be the first time that an insurance company gets thanked in a book like this, but while I was out of town researching, my pipes broke and my house flooded. Without the kindness and professionalism of USAA, much valuable writing time would have been lost to the process of drying out and repairing my house. And to my neighbor Cathie Herman, who realized what was happening and who turned my water off at the street, my undying gratitude. Because of her, nothing that mattered was damaged.

The time for writing was important but equally important was the time away from it. Those who made time for me and got me out of my head get my deepest thanks. Molly McCabe, Maren Parsons Richter, Jim and Laura Parsons, thank you. I always appreciate the time my family makes for me when I can get to them: so thanks Mom, Steve, Carolee, Amanda, Robert, and Philip. And thanks to Danette for a terrific time in DC. Locally, my life would be much less interesting without Beth Gylys, Tonia Edwards, Drew Nail, Rasha Ramzy, Jennifer Barker, Melissa Stafford, Holley Wilkin, Jennifer Chatman, Sergio Gallo, and David Cheshier.

No one has done more to teach me about things rhetorical as they pertain to the presidency than Marty Medhurst and David Zarefsky. This book is dedicated to them and expresses only a small part of the debt I and all those who study presidential rhetoric owe them both.

INTRODUCTION

COMMUNICATING THE PRESIDENCY

Running for re-election as the oldest president in history, Ronald Reagan knew that his age would be a campaign issue. Its importance was heightened by the fact that his opponent, Walter Mondale, was only 56 years old in 1984, and had significant experience, having served as both senator and vice-president. Asked about the age question during the second presidential debate, Reagan answered, "I will not make age an issue of this campaign. I am not going to exploit, for political purposes, my opponent's youth and inexperience." This apparently trivial quip demonstrated that at age 73, Reagan still had his wits about him and thus defused the age issue. This demonstration apparently trumped the numerous mistakes of fact and other verbal stumbles that were also part of Reagan's public performance during the 1984 campaign. Without ever making an actual argument or addressing the very real questions surrounding his age and mental capacities, Reagan's humor took the issue of his fitness for office off the political table. It was a masterful exhibition of rhetorical skill.

But it was not without precedent. In 1944, running for a previously unimaginable fourth term, a tired and increasingly frail Franklin D. Roosevelt faced similar questions about his fitness for office. He also refused to respond directly to such questions. He too defused them with humor. Taking the fight straight to the Republicans, FDR said,

> These Republican leaders have not been content with attacks on me, or my wife, or on my sons. No, not content with that, they now include my little dog, Fala. Well, of course, I don't

resent attacks, and my family doesn't resent attacks, but Fala does resent them. You know, Fala is Scotch, and being a Scottie, as soon as he learned that the Republican fiction writers in Congress and out had concocted a story that I had left him behind on the Aleutian Islands and had sent a destroyer back to find him—at a cost to the taxpayers of two or three, or eight or twenty million dollars—his Scotch soul was furious. He has not been the same dog since. I am accustomed to hearing malicious falsehoods about myself—such as that old, worm-eaten chestnut that I have represented myself as indispensable. But I think I have a right to resent, to object to libelous statements about my dog.

As with the Reagan example, Roosevelt here made an implicit case about his capacity to govern, arguing that unlike the Republicans, Roosevelt was focused on important, rather than trivial matters. He did not resent Republican attacks. The Republicans were depicted as malicious liars, desperate to discredit the president and all his works. They, unlike the president, could not be trusted.

Both Reagan's quip and Roosevelt's more extended narrative are the stuff of political rhetoric, and both these speakers have well-justified reputations for rhetorical ability. They wield emotion and tell stories. They imply arguments that are not fully articulated and that require audience involvement to complete. They tell us something about the political character of the presidents and their opposition. They support the presidents' claims to personal and institutional power. Neither of these examples are eloquent, reminding us that rhetorical skill is not always exhibited in soaring language. These examples made arguments without making them explicit and earned admiration without making a direct appeal for political support.

These appeals are widely considered to have helped these presidents win their campaigns and keep their jobs in the White House. But despite such examples, and despite the deep-rooted belief in the power of political words, "rhetoric" is one of the most frequently used—and misused—words in American politics. Presidential speeches are dismissed as "mere" rhetoric while being criticized for lacking eloquence. At the same time, presidents must be seen leading and heard speaking to be understood as leaders. Reagan and Roosevelt seemed presidential and were therefore assumed to be capable of governing. Their images were carefully cultivated, for presidential governance involves the creation and maintenance of ties to the mass public. These ties do not depend entirely on party affiliations and have a great deal to do with the person and personality of the chief executive. Presidents have always exercised public leadership, and both visual and verbal rhetoric have always been part of that leadership. But the rhetorical elements of leadership, like all of its other elements, have not always been exercised in the same ways. Rhetoric has not always offered the same kinds of opportunities over time, nor has it been subject to the same kinds of constraints. Presidents can learn from history, as Reagan surely did from the example set by Roosevelt, but they are unlikely to be able to replicate it.

The goal of this book, then, is to offer a review of the scholarship on the rhetorical presidency and presidential rhetoric, with an eye toward the ways in which our political history can help students of the presidency understand and practice the kinds of rhetoric that lends itself to both policy success and the facilitation of civic engagement and a healthy democracy. This introductory chapter begins with a very brief discussion of how "rhetoric" might be understood, then moves to an analysis of presidential rhetoric and the rhetorical presidency. That analysis includes work on the "permanent campaign" and how it has led presidents to the strategy of "going public," which is largely ineffective as a means of moving public opinion on narrowly defined issues in the short term. Having demonstrated what public communication is unlikely to help presidents accomplish, I then discuss the ways in which that communication might be more usefully understood and employed in the various exercises of presidential power. The chapter concludes with an overview of the rest of the book.

Rhetoric, Politics, and the Presidency

The study of rhetoric has been with us as long as the study of politics, and changes in one are reflected in changes in the other. When politics are understood, for instance, as the exercising power over the mass, rhetoric is persuasion—a mechanism through which the ..ul gain consent and legitimate their rule. When politics is understood in more democratic terms, however, we conceive of rhetoric less as simple persuasion and more as a complex process in which audiences as well as speakers have interpretive agency. The ways in which we understand the capacities of rhetoric, then, reflect and influence the ways in which we understand our shared political capacities.

Aristotle famously defined rhetoric as the marshaling of the "available means of persuasion," and in ancient times the study of rhetoric was closely tied to the analysis of rhetorical form with an eye toward making orators more persuasive. The idea here is that audiences are always persuadable. A speaker's job is to understand and make use of the opportunities inherent in a particular situation toward a persuasive end. This understanding of rhetoric is probably the one most people continue to think of as "rhetoric." It assumes that all the agency lies in the hands of a speaker whose goal is to change opinions more or less inertly residing in an audience. It is no surprise that adherents of this understanding of rhetoric are also suspicious of it and its practitioners, for the emphasis here is largely on the speaker's ability to move an audience regardless of the validity or morality of the claims being advanced. In its crudest form, this view of rhetoric implies that meaning is created by the speaker and either accepted or rejected by the audience. It is not a view that is easily sustainable given what we now know about persuasion and its limits.

Writing in more democratically-inflected times, Kenneth Burke understood rhetoric not as persuasion, but as identification. For Burke, all language is a means of connecting humans to one another. Rhetorical unity, for Burke, is required by the fact of social division. He understood rhetoric as less about persuading one's audience to a particular view of a matter, and more about finding ways to establish a kind of community with that audience. Speakers seeking to establish identification with their audiences employ what Burke called "terministic screens," or lenses through which the world can be understood. These terministic screens, or what we now think of as linguistic frames, are important aspects of political, especially presidential, rhetoric, for they are the mechanisms through which presidents exercise their most important rhetorical power, that of definition.

Because of their position as both head of state and as head of government, presidents, at least since FDR, are the clearest voices in our national politics, and they help us understand the broad political contexts in which they govern, setting individual policy decisions within those contexts. So when Roosevelt argued, for example, that the European War was best understood as a battle between good and evil, and when, years later, Dwight Eisenhower and Ronald Reagan made similar claims about the Cold War, those definitions were consequential both for American policy and for our national identity.

These claims, moreover, acted not just through definition, but also through association and dissociation. In defining World War II and later the Cold War in these terms, presidents also divided the political world, associating the United States and its allies with certain concepts (good, God, light) and separating the United States and its allies from other concepts (evil, godlessness, darkness). These terms relied on and contributed to our national self-understanding as "exceptional," with a divinely ordained mission in the world, and thus lent authority to some policies while ensuring that others could not be seriously considered. At the same time, they helped legitimate the assumption of political power by the national government and the chief executive. These were, of course, political processes. They are simultaneously rhetorical processes.

While political scientists, following Aristotle, often rely on the classical view of rhetoric as a set of tools designed to persuade, rhetoricians, following Burke, tend to view rhetoric as more contingent, involving a complex interaction of context, specific choices made by the speaker, and situated audience interpretations of those choices. In this context, the power presidents wield is also a contingent mixture of institutional authority and technical acumen. When successful, this power largely resides in the president's ability to offer definitions that influence how audiences understand their shared social reality. Once the social world is defined, important political questions are also structured, potential responses are shaped, and institutional capacities for action are authorized. It is important to note, however, that not all presidential definitions are accepted by significant national audiences. The power of definition, like all rhetoric, is socially interactive. Presidents do not unilaterally control the frames of our national politics. When successful, they articulate frames that already find some kind of public resonance.

So when FDR promised a "New Deal" for the nation's "forgotten man," he was also making an argument about the causes and consequences of the Hoover administration's policies. When George W. Bush connected the attacks on September 11, 2001, to an "Axis of Evil," he too was making an argument about the causes and consequences of those attacks. Neither definition was unanimously accepted, but both maintained enough cultural and political currency to authorize massive governmental action. The same cannot, however, be said for Gerald Ford's efforts to mobilize the nation around his "Whip Inflation Now" campaign or for Jimmy Carter's attempt to fight national "malaise." Both of these latter policy programs may have been useful to the nation, but neither found the public resonance needed to authorize political action.

That resonance can be located in both rhetoric understood as words and rhetoric understood as images. In addition to the tradition of analyzing spoken and written texts, there is an increasingly important body of work dedicated to the analysis of visual argumentation. For our purposes, this means that not only are presidential words important elements in the presentation of political arguments, but so are the images that accompany those words. The artifacts with which presidents surround themselves in the Oval Office, the staging of their events, and the juxtaposition of historical markers all make implicit political arguments. When a president places a bust of Theodore Roosevelt or a portrait of George Washington in the Oval Office, he is associating his administration with the values connected to those men. These arguments can reflect common understandings of the things that "belong" together, and thus they channel ideologies. They are not necessarily always reflective of intentional actions by conscious actors.

Finally, a president's capacity to assume and extend political power interacts with popular culture. Films such as *Gabriel over the White House* offered a vision of a strong chief executive in the 1930s. More recently, depictions of the president exemplify the ambivalence with which we regard political power—presidents are heroic (*Air Force One, Independence Day*), malevolent (*Executive Power*), and wisely foolish (*Dave*). The range of opinions about political power is evident by a quick look at the way it is depicted in two very popular television shows: *The West Wing* presents political power very differently than *House of Cards*. Fictional portrayals of the president and political power can redound to the actual president's advantage—especially when she is envisioned as heroic—but can also help create and maintain unrealistic expectations of the capacities of the office and of its occupant. Furthermore, portrayals of the chief executive as venal can also help undermine the political legitimacy of the institution and its occupant. Depictions of the president as a fool do not do much for her or his public image, either, as the famous caricature of Gerald Ford on *Saturday Night Live* illustrates. Ford, that most athletic of presidents, is firmly embedded in public memory as clumsy, thanks to Chevy Chase. Presidents associate themselves with their heroic predecessors—the figures of Washington, Lincoln, and Jefferson are more common in the West Wing than those of Nixon or Fillmore, for example. Efforts to make the president seem heroic can backfire, however. Surely, when George W. Bush landed on an aircraft carrier in a flight suit and spoke in front of a banner declaring "Mission Accomplished," no one in his administration anticipated the ways in which those images would be recirculated as the war in Iraq dragged endlessly on.

As these examples indicate, all of the ways presidents present themselves and their institution are forms of presidential rhetoric and are thus subject to rhetorical analysis. Rhetoric has always pervaded the presidency but the ways in which that history might best be understood and put to contemporary use are a matter of some debate. That debate centers, in large part, around the constructs of presidential rhetoric and the rhetorical presidency.

Presidential Rhetoric and the Rhetorical Presidency

There are three main ways of apprehending the rhetorical power of the presidency. First, that power can be understood as instrumental—words are taken at their face value and the assumption is that rhetoric is aimed at facilitating specific policy proposals. Most political agency is located in an individual president who makes linguistic choices aimed at a narrowly defined and specific end. Most presidents, it should be noted, appear to agree with and operate under this understanding of rhetoric. So when FDR, to return to an earlier example, argued for heightened US involvement in Europe, he sought language that was most likely to convince people to change their minds about the nature of that war. The focus of this understanding is on persuasion, generally understood as opinion change.

A second approach to presidential rhetoric, however, understands these choices as significantly constrained by national ideologies and thinks of rhetoric as at least potentially constitutive. Language is both wielded by speakers and speaks through them—what appear to be "choices" are constrained by the overall ideology in which the speakers are embedded. When applied to the presidency, this view implies that presidential rhetoric, because it occurs in a locus of institutional power, both reflects and creates the dominant ideology among its audiences. Rhetoric is less important as a mover of public opinion on specific issues and more important as a creator of a particular kind of public, which will therefore "naturally" hold certain opinions.

But we can understand these two positions as points on a continuum, giving us a third way to understand the capacity of political rhetoric. It is probably most useful to apprehend language as both instrumental and constitutive and look to the ways it may both help gain an instrumental goal and also have constitutive consequences. Such consequences may be apparent in the definitions, associations, and dissociations a president uses over time, and can rarely if ever be seen as opinion change following a specific single speech. So to again return to my earlier example, depictions of the United States as exceptional, as associated with the divinely ordained forces of light at perpetual war with the forces of darkness, have a long history. That history made specific ideas and images available to FDR and later to the Cold War presidents. Presidential rhetoric, while wielded by individuals and always inflected by individual practice, is also importantly institutional and ideological, and should be understood in all of these ways. The institutional context of presidential rhetoric is particularly important in structuring that rhetoric.

The Contemporary Context

Presidential rhetoric, like presidential politics more generally, has of course changed over time. Because my focus here is on contemporary practice, I will not treat that history here, but start with the most important recent developments. The Reagan presidency brought with it both changes in the practices of and scholarship on governance. Ronald Reagan became president at the same time that changes in media technologies began accelerating. The confluence of his style with those changes also helped further trends that were increasingly apparent in national politics, especially a reliance on the relationship between the president and the people; the modern mass media; and changes in electoral practices. These changes combined to transform the institution of the presidency and thus all of American politics. Many scholars argue that these changes replaced public deliberation among elites with mass persuasion, altering the balance of power between Congress and the presidency and putting members of both institutions at the mercy of an uninformed mass public who were easily swayed by the machinations of popular leaders. They sometimes argue, therefore, that the solution to this problem is a reduction in the length of campaigns, a reduction in the number of speeches given by presidents, who should also eschew "inspirational rhetoric." Here, the suspicion of public rhetoric apparent in the ancients is very much on display. Sometimes these arguments seem to make the case that government is best left to elites. More often, the proponents of these ideas are worried that focusing national attention on the person of the president rather than the substance of policy is bad for what we now call "civic engagement," and thus bad for democratic government, not least because it replaced attention to issues with a focus on personality.

This historical trajectory of increased presidential power as a result of more media and thus a focus on the person of the president can be found at least as far back as the 1930s. These trends, including structural changes and the development of the mass media, meant that elections—and thus national politics— had become more shallowly personal than deeply political. Some scholars believe that the investments the mass public made in politics were connected to the person of the president rather than the politics she espoused, and that consequently, citizens had ever higher hopes of what presidents could do. Those hopes were placed on institutional structures that had no chance of fulfilling them, inevitably first leading to disappointment, and then to a search for a better person with better promises. The burden the cycle places on the system and on the individual president are both immense and unrealistic, leading to a pathological politics. The presidency now has advantages Congress lacks when treating with the mass public. Those advantages, however, do not translate into more power or to the better use of the power already accrued by the institution and its denizens.

American governance is more centered on the chief executive than it once was. But it is important to remember that there was never a time in which our national politics were largely deliberative and issue-based. Our national political history and political language have always been composed of a mixture of what Aristotle labeled the epideictic, deliberative, and forensic modes. Rhetoricians who study the presidency also argue that these modes are not mutually exclusive, but that even speeches geared toward ceremonial ends can have substantive content and consequences. For those who take rhetoric seriously, it can be a useful lens into the practices of national politics. As those politics change, so do the form and functions of the rhetoric that helps structure and legitimate those practices.

Regardless of how one views national political history and the rhetoric that defines it, there is agreement that presidential candidates, faced with an increasingly complicated and fractious electorate, consistently escalate the promises they make to that electorate, and thus consistently deepen the cycle of high expectations. Seeking to fulfill those promises, and unable to control, much less to command, Congress, presidents continually seek increased leverage over the policy process. They have hoped to find it in the strategy of what Samuel Kernell calls "going public." When presidents go public, they not only speak to the mass public; they also ask citizens to pressure their representatives and senators, urging action on a specific piece of legislation. This meant that presidents, who once faced the mass public rarely and then increasingly campaigned publicly, now govern in public and with the authority and impetus of public opinion behind them. Presidential authority now also means public legitimacy. Presidents, however, who sought to wield public opinion to further their own agendas ended by having to answer to the public as well. This situation, dubbed the "permanent campaign," characterizes the contemporary era, where presidents who hoped to use the public as leverage over Congress are now trapped by the expectation that they will be constantly before the public. Presidents who thought to increase their political power by establishing apparently intimate relationships with the public are now prisoners of that relationship. On top of that, there is evidence that the strategies associated with going public may not provide the benefits presidents hoped for them and the cost they pay may not be worth the benefits they reap.

The Case against Rhetoric: Going Public and the Politics of Short-Term Opinion Change

It is easy to argue that presidential rhetoric doesn't matter, if by that we mean that it has the power to change public opinion in the short term. We live in a time of heightened partisanship, in which it seems that increasingly few people listen to opposing arguments, much less find themselves persuaded by them. We also live in hyper-mediated era, in which citizens can pick and choose their forms of news and entertainment, and may not be exposed to viewpoints that differ from their own. Having decided, for whatever reason, to oppose a president, a citizen may easily avoid hearing any arguments in that president's favor and may equally easily avoid hearing directly from the president as well.

Presidents may have a similar problem when it comes to persuading Congress. No scholar has done more to demonstrate that rhetoric is ineffective than George C. Edwards, III. Over the course of several books and numerous essays, Edwards has argued that if presidential persuasion matters at all, it matters only "at the margins" of congressional activity. He argues that presidents make a mistake when they abandon bargaining with Congress for "going public" and demonstrates that even the presidents we most associate with rhetorical acumen failed to alter public opinion on the issues that mattered most to them, and argues that presidents would have greater success facilitating their policy agendas by "staying private" and capitalizing on existing public opinion rather than wasting time and energy trying to alter that opinion and attempting to direct it toward leveraging congressional action. This understanding of the limits of presidential persuasion depends upon a narrow view of rhetoric, and confines presidential communication to targeted speech designed to promote change in public opinion. It is thus not very surprising that there is little evidence of such change as a result of single speeches. There is also little evidence that the mass public can be easily motivated to pressure Congress as a result of presidential encouragement to do so. Public opinion is not easily moved, and the mass public is unlikely to be motivated to exert the kind of pressure "going public" demands. But public speech actually has different kinds of consequences presidents would do well to consider.

The Case for Rhetoric: Legitimating Governance

First, and most obviously, there is the capacity of presidential discourses (as opposed to single speeches) to alter public understandings of an issue. This capacity cannot be measured by studies of short-term public opinion, but can be seen in long-term changes over time in how important the mass public may consider an issue, or in how presidential definitions may be caught up and carried over various media. There is good evidence that the more attention a president gives to an issue, especially in such major speeches as the State of the Union Address, the more attention the media give that issue. Presidents may not be able to alter public opinion on an issue in the short term, but they can affect the amount of attention given to that issue, and they can influence the public understanding of it.

Second, as Karlyn Kohrs Campbell and Kathleen Hall Jamieson demonstrate, rhetoric not only defines the political context, but helps create institutional capacities for political action. By positioning themselves as they do vis-à-vis the other branches of government and the American people, by interpreting national politics and national political life as they do, presidents collectively create the institution, stretching and constraining its capacity to act. Presidents must concern themselves not only with power, but also with authority, or the capacity for present and future action. Rhetoric can be an important factor in the legitimation of that authority.

Third, presidents may actually get more benefit from public appearances than it may appear. We know that "going local" does pay off in terms of terms of both positive newspaper coverage and public opinion. Presidents sometimes do have some success in public persuasion, and that this success may depend upon the degree and extent of opposition. Going public may not affect national public opinion, but it might very well matter in specific districts. Changes at the margins may matter a great deal in closely fought battles.

Fourth, presidents who go public may not actually have the public as their only, or even their primary audience. They may be using ostensibly public rhetoric to signal their policy preferences to other elites. Presidents, perhaps even more than other kinds of speakers, speak to multiple audiences simultaneously and may have multiple goals in doing so. Presidential relationships with public opinion are complicated, and may not always be geared toward change. Presidents might well be invested in maintaining public opinion, in activating certain aspects of it while minimizing other aspects, in appearing to be led rather than in leading. Presidents have considerably more success leading public opinion under some conditions, and are generally more willing to rely on public opinion when it is consistent with their preferences than when it differs with those preferences. So it may be misleading to consider presidential rhetoric only through the lens of the capacity of a single speech to alter public opinion.

Fifth, presidents, even when they may not attain their own policy goals, may still be leaving behind them a set of inventional resources for their successors. Harry Truman, for instance, could not persuade either Congress or the mass public to his way of thinking on national medical insurance, but his arguments returned with greater resonance under different political circumstances, and it is revealing that he signed the bill at the White House; Truman was the first person enrolled in Medicare. More contemporarily, politicians on the right continue to claim Ronald Reagan as the progenitor of their policy choices, and his rhetorical legacies are lasting in all kinds of ways, some more credible than others. The presidency, like the Supreme Court, is a self-referential institution, and presidents who appear to have fallen short in their own time nevertheless leave political and rhetorical resources behind them.

Finally, presidents serve an important representative function. They muster and create symbolic resources that unite the nation and that connect it to the national past as well as projecting it into the possible future. Presidents, as national representatives, interpret the nation both domestically and internationally, and this act of "speaking for" is as important as the act of "speaking to." As the institution developed, the relationship between the president and the people altered from a distant, removed, and largely administrative relationship into one of close personal attachment and national representation. From the founding to presidents like Andrew Jackson and Abraham Lincoln, who were in some senses aberrations, to the more routinized changes associated with Woodrow Wilson and Theodore Roosevelt, and then the solidification of the personalized presidency under the administration of Franklin

Roosevelt, and the increased reliance on public politics, presidents have come to represent the nation in ways that altered both presidential rhetoric and the institutions of the national government.

Just as it matters which nations a president chooses to visit and which to slight on international trips, presidents send powerful messages of inclusion and exclusion at home simply by the act of visiting some places and not others, of addressing some audiences and not others. These are not "merely symbolic" choices, but powerful implicit statements about the composition and direction of the nation. They are statements that only a president is empowered to make.

The Power of Presidential Rhetoric

Presidential rhetoric, then, is best understood as a particular kind of tool facilitating certain aspects of executive authority. Rhetoric is a twofold practice, engaged in by both speakers and their audiences. For speakers, rhetoric is a way of creating audiences, establishing connections with them, and representing them. For audiences, rhetoric is a way of understanding the terms and conditions of the relationships speakers establish with them. When a president declares that as Americans, "we" believe in certain values and those values mandate certain kinds of political action, she is also declaring that "we" are a certain kind of people who stand in a specific relationship to the president and to the policies she espouses. When the public interprets, accepts, or rejects that proposition, it is also engaging in rhetoric. There is not a simple, straight line between the messages presidents send, the messages audiences receive, and the consequences of those messages. Instead, presidents and their audiences engage in a complex dance of meaning and interpretation. Power differentials, however, matter. Presidents have power their mass audiences do not, but the mass public is not without interpretive power either. The dance of democracy, then, is a rhetorical one, structured by institutions and by the power relationships those institutions embody.

Presidential speech matters as well, although not in a simple or easily measured way. So does presidential silence. Both reveal the capacities of presidents to speak to us a nation, to represent us as a nation, to channel our national hopes and dreams, and to make them concrete in the form of policy. Presidents tell us who we are, and also who we are not—they offer visions of inclusion and also tell us who are excluded from the national polity. Presidents articulate ideologies as well as policies, and in the process they reaffirm and challenge the values and beliefs that unite us a nation. Presidents, through their public speech, thus access and influence the symbolic dimensions of national politics.

Some of these dimensions are reflected in the style and frequency of their speech. From the florid discourses of the nineteenth century to the more conversational and even anti-intellectual style of the politicians currently favor, presidents suit their style to the culture they govern. That adaptation, of course, has consequences. The scholars of the "personal presidency" and the "rhetorical presidency" were not wrong in their observations that our national politics has become unbalanced, and that the imbalance puts stresses on the system. They were not wrong in noting that this imbalance is associated with the creation of a broader, more inclusive polity that was facilitated by the New Deal and Franklin D. Roosevelt's political practices. Scholars are incorrect, however, in assuming that prior to Roosevelt (or Wilson) the presidency was somehow less rhetorical or even more deliberative. Presidents, it is true, talked to a smaller section of the mass public. That talk was necessarily different than it became when the electorate changed. But those changes were driven as much by the nature of the polity as by the nature of presidential speech.

But changes in the national audience also meant changes in presidential speech. Partly, this has to do with changes in the media environment. As the media became more dependent on visuals, presidents began to provide those visuals. When presidents talk in order to be understood as leading, then that talk becomes at once trivialized and magnified. It becomes trivialized because it occurs so often. Presidential words have less weight when they seem to speak on everything all of the time. The presidency itself seems to have less of an aura of remoteness and thus of grandeur; it is a more democratized office in many ways. But the expectation that presidents will speak with eloquence and import is with us still.

Presidential speech is in some ways trivialized, but it is also magnified, as everything a president says or does becomes a potential topic of national debate (think of Barack Obama's "selfie" at Nelson Mandela's funeral, for example). When the media are less hierarchically structured, the "gatekeeping" function of deciding what is "news" becomes diminished, and public attention can wander seemingly randomly from policy debates to the celebrity aspects of the chief executive and his family and staff and back again with no apparent rationale. Presidents often appear to float on the media stream rather than being able to direct it. But the expectation of control and direction remain.

Presidents could once exercise some command over the national stage, although I suspect that this command was more limited and partial than we sometimes assume. Certainly they now share the stage with an ever increasing number of voices, from members of Congress to the chattering classes, bloggers, citizen-journalists, and seemingly everyone on Twitter. Presidents still speak more loudly and garner more attention than most political actors. Yet it can be hard for a president to control the "national narrative" or "win the news cycle" when there are always multiple narratives, the news cycle is apparently endless, and the number of competing voices escalates every day. But the expectation that the president can and should direct a single national political conversation remains.

When presidents think that they can facilitate short-term policy change by simply talking, they are, in many if not most cases, focusing their attention in the wrong place. With the increased competition and the number of narratives that circle around any important policy issue, with the increased size, complexity, and fractiousness of the national polity, it is asking a lot of any single political tactic to forge changes in that vast and inchoate entity we think of as "national public opinion." As numerous political scientists have indicated, speech making alone is not sufficient to create such changes in the short term. And presidents, by the nature of the office, are fixated on the short term. But presidents who fail to engage the public in the course of policy debates are ceding the part of the national stage they still control to their opposition. Presidents who refuse to offer definitions to the public will be at the mercy of the definitions offered by others. Engaging in public oratory does not guarantee success in national policy debates, but neglecting this aspect of the job practically guarantees failure, as George H. W. Bush found after the 1989 California earthquake, and as George W. Bush discovered after Hurricane Katrina in 2005. Neglecting the institution's rhetorical responsibilities will inevitably diminish its political capacities as well.

Presidents who neglect the rhetorical aspects of their job also neglect, in large part, their obligation to represent the American people. No other political figure has the president's ability to speak for the nation, to call upon, in Abraham Lincoln's phrase, "the better angels of our nature," to tell us who we are and who we aspire to be. More importantly, when presidents ignore the capacity of their public speech to constitute the public, they miss opportunities to make their larger case to the American people in ways that connect values, national identity, and policy. If the effectiveness of presidential rhetoric is to be understood as defining national audiences and articulating national identity in ways that facilitate certain kinds of policy choices while foreclosing others and in creating in the executive office the capacity to act based on those definitions, then practitioners of that rhetoric must be both consistent and patient. They must be able to offer definitions that move the nation in the direction that they want it moved while recognizing that such movement is unlikely in the short time frame available to them. Presidents must use even the smallest occasions to make the largest of points. And they must, above all, recognize that rhetoric is a single tactic available to them. Poor public speech will generate all kinds of problems for them that "good" speech, however defined, will be unable to solve. In rhetoric, as in the institution more generally, recognizing limits is both very difficult and absolutely essential.

Plan of the Book

The rest of this briefing book lays out the ways in which we might usefully understand the capacities and limitations of presidential rhetoric. The first chapter argues that presidents must be seen in order to be understood as governing; an invisible president is a president who is surrendering leverage over the national agenda to other political actors. Drawing on lessons from various administrations, this chapter treats the ways in which presidents can—and cannot—influence that agenda, and how they might best accommodate the requirements of the contemporary media environment, with the demands of the twenty-four hour news cycle, the fragmented nature of the national media and the growth of narrowcasting.

The second chapter locates presidential rhetoric as both distinctively individual and profoundly institutional. Beginning with the founding period, when the president's personal voice went largely unheard except through the indirect mediation of surrogates and the partisan press through the "rise of the rhetorical presidency," the growth of the "personal presidency," and the strategies associated with "going public." In the context of those developments this chapter goes into questions of "authenticity"; the role of speechwriters and surrogates and how to make the best use of both; the uses and dangers of press conferences and other rhetorical opportunities; and it addresses the ways in which presidents can make the best use of their larger messaging structures such as the White House Office of Communication.

The president's changed relationship with the people and thus also with Congress has provided the president with both challenges and opportunities. The argument of chapter 3 focuses on some of those challenges and opportunities, and alerts presidents to the ways in which they might take advantage of both. The chapter includes discussions of ways in which presidents can take advantage of commemorative and other ceremonial events to frame larger issues and events; the opportunities inherent in the State of the Union and other routine high-profile rhetorical moments; and ways to minimize the dangers inherent in gaffes and scandal.

The Conclusion discusses both the historical development of presidential rhetoric and the institutionalized mechanisms associated with the rhetorical presidency. It concludes by noting that while rhetoric is not especially effective in changing public opinion in the short term, it is a way in which presidents can affect the national agenda, fulfill their representative function, encourage civic engagement, and frame national issues over the long term. Of particular interest here is the ability of presidents to define national identity quite broadly and political issues more narrowly. The chapter concludes with a brief discussion of what, given the findings of the briefing book constitutes "good" rhetoric, and how presidents might engage in "good" rhetorical practices.

Suggestions for Further Reading

Anderson, Karrin Vasby, and Kristy Horn Sheeler. *Woman President: Confronting Postfeminist Political Culture.* College Station: Texas A&M University Press, 2013.

Beasley, Vanessa. *You, the People: American National Identity in Presidential Rhetoric.* College Station: Texas A&M University Press, 2004.

Burke, Kenneth. *A Rhetoric of Motives.* Berkeley: University of California Press, 1969.

Ceaser, James W., Glen E. Thurow, Jeffrey K. Tulis, and Joseph M. Besette, "The Rise of the Rhetorical Presidency." *Presidential Studies Quarterly* 11 (1981): 158–71.

Campbell, Karlyn Kohrs, and Kathleen Hall Jamieson, *Presidents Creating the Presidency: Deeds Done in Words.* Chicago: University of Chicago Press, 2008.

Cohen, Jeffrey E. "Presidential Rhetoric and the Public Agenda." *American Journal of Political Science* 39 (1995): 87–107.

Cohen, Jeffrey E. *Going Local: Presidential Leadership in the Post-Broadcast Age.* Cambridge: Cambridge University Press, 2009.

Cummins, Jeff. "The President's Domestic Agenda, Divided Government, and the Relationship to the Public Agenda." *American Review of Politics* 27 (2006): 269–94.

Cummins, Jeff. "State of the Union Addresses and the President's Legislative Success." *Congress & the Presidency* 37 (2010): 176–99.

Edwards, George C., III. *At the Margins: Presidential Leadership of Congress.* New Haven: Yale University Press, 1989.

Edwards, George C., III. *On Deaf Ears.* New Haven: Yale University Press, 2003.

Edwards, George C., III. *The Strategic President: Persuasion and Opportunity in Presidential Leadership.* Princeton: Princeton University Press, 2009.

Entman, Robert M. "Cascading Activation: Contesting the White House's Frame after 9/11." *Political Communication* 20 (2003): 413–32.

Esbaugh-Soha, Matthew. *The President's Speeches: Beyond "Going Public."* Boulder, CO: Lynne Reiner Publishers, 2006.

Finnegan, Cara. "Picturing the President: Obama and the Visual Politics of White House Art." In *The Rhetoric of Heroic Expectations: Establishing the Obama Presidency,* edited by Justin Vaughan and Jennifer Mercieca, 209–34. College Station: Texas A&M University Press, 2014.

Goodale, Greg. "The Presidential Sound: From Orotund to Instructional Speech, 1892–1912." *Quarterly Journal of Speech* 96 (2010): 164–84.

Gross, David. *The Secret History of Emotion: From Aristotle's Rhetoric to Modern Brain Science.* Chicago: University of Chicago Press, 2007.

Hager, Gregory L., and Terry Sullivan. "President-Centered and Presidency-Centered Explanations of Presidential Public Activity." *American Journal of Political Science* 38, no. 4 (1994): 1079–1103.

Han, Lori Cox, and Diane J. Heith. *In the Public Domain: Presidents and the Challenges of Public Leadership.* New York: SUNY Press, 2005.

Hart, Roderick P. *The Sound of Leadership: Presidential Communication in the Modern Age.* Chicago: University of Chicago Press, 1989.

Hart, Roderick P. *Seducing America: How Television Charms the Modern Voter.* Thousand Oaks, CA: Sage, 1998.

Hart, Roderick P., Jay P. Childers, and Colene J. Lind. *Political Tone: How Leaders Talk and Why.* Chicago: University of Chicago Press, 2013.

Hemmings, Clare. "Invoking Affect: Cultural Theory and the Ontological Turn." *Cultural Studies* 19 (2005): 548–67.

Hoffman, Karen S. *Popular Leadership in the Presidency: Origins and Practices.* Lanham, MD: Lexington Books, 2010.

Ivie, Robert L. "Images of Savagery in American Justifications for War." *Communications Monographs* 47, no. 4 (1980): 279–94.

Jamieson, Kathleen Hall. *Packaging the Presidency.* 3rd ed. New York: Oxford University Press, 1996.

Jamieson, Kathleen Hall. *Eloquence in an Electronic Age: The Transformation of Political Speechmaking.* New York: Oxford University Press, 1990.

Keith, William M., and Christian O. Lundberg. *The Essential Guide to Rhetoric.* Boston: Bedford/St. Martin's, 2008.

Kernell, Samuel. *Going Public: New Strategies of Presidential Leadership.* 4th ed. Washington, DC: CQ Press, 2006.

Laracey, Mel. *Presidents and the People; The Partisan Story of Going Public.* College Station: Texas A&M University Press, 2010.

Lim, Elvin T. "Five Trends in Presidential Rhetoric: An Analysis of Rhetoric from George Washington to Bill Clinton," *Presidential Studies Quarterly* 32 (2002): 228–45.

Lim, Elvin T. The Presidency and the Media: Two Faces of Democracy." In *The Presidency and the Political System*, 10th ed., edited by Michael Nelson, 258–71. Washington, DC: CQ Press, 2013.

Lowi, Theodore J. *The Personal Presidency: Power Invested, Promise Unfulfilled.* Ithaca: Cornell University Press, 1985.

Maltese, John Anthony. *Spin Control: The White House Office of Communication and the Management of Presidential News.* Charlotte: University of North Carolina Press, 1994.

Mayer, Jeremy D. "The Presidency and Image Management: Discipline in Search of Illusion." *Presidential Studies Quarterly* 34 (2004): 620–31.

Medhurst, Martin J. ed. *Beyond the Rhetorical Presidency.* College Station: Texas A&M University Press, 1996.

Osborn, Michael. "Archetypal Metaphor in Rhetoric: The Light-Dark Family." *Quarterly Journal of Speech* 53, no. 2 (1967): 115–26.

Osborn, Michael. "The Evolution of the Archetypal Sea in Rhetoric and Poetic." *Quarterly Journal of Speech* 63 (1977), 347–63.

Osborn, Michael. "The Trajectory of My Work with Metaphor." *Southern Communication Journal* 74, no. 1 (January–March 2009): 79–87.

Osborn, Michael, and Douglas Ehninger. "Metaphor in Public Address." *Speech Monographs* 29 (1962): 223–34.

Parry-Giles, Shawn, and Trevor Parry-Giles. *Constructing Clinton: Hyperreality and Presidential Image-Making in Postmodern Politics.* New York: Peter Lang, 2002.

Parry-Giles, Trevor, and Shawn Parry-Giles, "The *West Wing*'s Primetime Presidentiality: Mimesis and Catharsis in a Postmodern Romance." *Quarterly Journal of Speech* 88 (2002): 209–27.

Prelli, Lawrence J. *Rhetorics of Display.* Columbia: University of South Carolina Press, 2006.

Riley, Denise. *Impersonal Passion: Language as Affect.* Durham, NC: Duke University Press, 2005.

Ritter, Kurt, and Martin J. Medhurst, eds. *Presidential Speechwriting: From the New Deal to the Reagan Revolution and Beyond.* College Station: Texas A&M University Press, 2004.

Roochnik, David. *Of Art and Wisdom: Plato's Understanding of Techne.* University Park: Pennsylvania State University Press, 2007.

Rottinghaus, Brandon. *The Provisional Pulpit: Modern Presidential Leadership of Public Opinion.* College Station: Texas A&M University Press, 2010.

Shogan, Colleen J. *The Moral Rhetoric of American Presidents.* College Station: Texas A&M University Press, 2006.

Stuckey, Mary E. *Defining Americans: The Presidency and National Identity.* Lawrence: University Press of Kansas, 2004.

Stuckey, Mary E. "Rethinking the Rhetorical Presidency and Presidential Rhetoric." *Review of Communication* 10 (2010): 38–52.

Stuckey, Mary E., and Greg M. Smith, "The Presidency and Popular Culture," In *The Presidency, the Public, and the Parties,* edited by Michael Nelson, 211–21. Washington, DC: CQ Press, 2007.

Tenpas, Katherine Dunn. "The State of the Union Address." In . *The President's Words: Speeches and Speechmaking in the Modern White House,* edited by Michael Nelson and R. L. Riley, 147–205. Lawrence: University Press of Kansas, 2010.

Towle, Michael J. *Out of Touch: The Presidency and Public Opinion.* College Station: Texas A&M University Press, 2004.

Toye, Richard. *Rhetoric: A Very Short Introduction.* New York: Oxford University Press, 2013.

Tulis, Jeffrey K. *The Rhetorical Presidency.* Princeton: Princeton University Press, 1987.

Vaughn Justin A., and Jose D. Villalobos, "Conceptualizing and Measuring White House Staff Influence on Presidential Rhetoric." *Presidential Studies Quarterly* 36 (2006): 681–88.

Worthington, Ian, ed. *Persuasion: Greek Rhetoric in Action.* New York: Routledge, 2002.

Zarefsky, David. "Presidential Rhetoric and the Power of Definition." *Presidential Studies Quarterly* 34 (2004): 607–19.

Zarefsky, David. *President Johnson's War on Poverty: Rhetoric and History.* Tuscaloosa: University of Alabama Press, 1986.

ONE

THE PUBLIC, THE MEDIA, AND THE PRESIDENCY

Roughly three weeks before signing a proclamation pardoning Richard M. Nixon "for all offenses against the United States which he . . . has committed or may have committed," President Gerald R. Ford spoke to the Veterans of Foreign Wars (VFW) in Chicago, Illinois. Ford had been president for five days, taking the Oath of Office on August 12, 1974, following Nixon's resignation. In one of his first acts as president, Ford declared his intention to throw "the weight of my Presidency into the scales of justice on the side of leniency" and pardon at least some of those who had evaded the draft and refused to serve in Vietnam. The decision to offer conditional amnesty to draft evaders was not unexpected, although it was certainly controversial. What interests us here, however, is not just the controversy attending the decision but also the choice to announce it to the VFW, a group highly unlikely to support the president's policy. In deciding to face a presumptively hostile audience, the president earned some praise for political courage while potentially taking some of the controversial edge off the announcement. His real audience, then, was the media and the American people. The immediate audience served his larger purpose of conveying a particular kind of image to those larger audiences.

As in this case, it is always true that presidents have to think of their rhetoric in terms of a complicated set of audiences. Good speakers adapt their speech to their audiences, both identifying with them and wielding that sense of identification to the speaker's ends, often through association and dissociation—dividing the audience from some values, beliefs, and policies and attaching them to others. Because of the centrality of audience to

1

rhetorical practices, this chapter offers both historical and analytic overviews of relationship between the president, the mass public, and the role of political rhetoric in that relationship. The theme of this chapter is change and stability. Many scholars argue that during the twentieth century, changes in communication technology altered the way the nation was governed. Presidents, most notably Theodore Roosevelt, Woodrow Wilson, Franklin D. Roosevelt, Ronald Reagan, Bill Clinton, and perhaps Barack Obama, were able to master the technologies of their day and forge a particular kind of relationship with the mass public. Because that relationship is largely extra-institutional, however, it modifies the politics of presidential governance but has little effect on the institutional arrangements in which that governance is embedded. But once presidents began to routinely emphasize their relationship with the mass public as part of their leadership strategy, they began to govern in public and with public opinion as defined and measured by polls. Despite changes in context and technology, however, the underlying logic of presidential communication has remained stable.

Shifting to more public aspects of the office, some scholars argue, deemphasized private negotiation. This shift from private to public accompanied a similar shift from elite to mass-based politics, brought about by a combination of developing communication technologies and an expanded electorate. This chapter discusses the contours of these shifts, focusing on the ways they have changed the presidency as part of the political system and what this means in terms of the institution's more stable rhetorical practices. Beginning with the transformations wrought by Franklin D. Roosevelt's administration and continuing into the contemporary era, the chapter points to the ways in which many things have changed but the underlying logic of presidential communication has remained the same.

The Public Presidency

Scholars associate a multitude of changes with the persona and practices of Franklin D. Roosevelt. But it is also worth noting that many of the political and rhetorical changes we attribute to him were broad in scope and that Roosevelt, whose organizational ability and personal magnetism were unquestionable, was not alone in wielding either talent. Politics in the 1930s were changing, and they were doing so nationally, not just in the Oval Office. Many of these changes had begun prior to Roosevelt's presidency. While many things may have changed in the 1930s, the practices of campaigning did not really alter all that much—the election cycle was still very short, and patronage rather than public politics was the rule. Politics in the 1930s was still very much about elites—parties were stronger, and also less democratic, than they are now; political power was more clearly defined and more clearly structured. State party leaders, for instance, exercised significant power over national party nominations, and had considerable responsibilities in terms of getting out the vote and other electoral activities.

Beginning with the Roosevelt administration, however, politics began to shift. These changes, usually discussed as "candidate-centered politics," became routine by the 1980s and altered both campaigns and governance, diminishing the role of parties in both processes. Two things contributed to the shift from an emphasis on party organization to more ad hoc organizations focused on specific candidates. The first of these is television. Because of the ways television changed political imperatives, the argument goes, pre-television candidates and presidents such as Harry Truman, who owed his career first to the machinations of the Pendergast machine and then to the organizational politics of the Senate Democrats, would have virtually no chance in running a successful modern presidential campaign. Television undoubtedly contributed to the weakening of political parties and facilitated the growth of a politics that included a sense of the visual, but it is easy to overestimate this effect. James A. Farley, for instance, chair of the Democratic National Committee under Roosevelt and long-time political activist, wrote an undated essay on the "New Breed of Politician" that is worth quoting at length:

> In terms of our own history, I cannot conceive of much fundamental change, had the present means of communication been available in 1776. Indeed, for the true greats of our past,

they would have made things easier. The granite character of George Washington, which in my opinion is the corner-stone in our Republic's founding, would have been illuminated, not diminished by television. I cannot imagine Klieg lights dimming the fire in Andrew Jackson's eye, nor the fiercest artificial lights obliterating the majestic composure of Abraham Lincoln's mighty spirit. President Theodore Roosevelt's tremendous energy would have been more than a match for an electric machine, and Woodrow Wilson's austere purity would have been conveyed as stemming from the pulse of the deeply human heart within it.

I think the old-time stem-winding orators wouldn't last five minutes today. People today want facts and decision in a terse half-hour, not a four hour exercise in metaphors and similes. In my own time, Franklin Delano Roosevelt changed all that with his radio fireside chats. The voice was great to be sure, but the public sensed that behind it was an even greater heart. And, as has been elsewhere said, what comes from the heart goes to the heart, whether by radio, TV, or newspaper.

For Farley, then, good politics relies on people of good public character, and this character would be clear to audiences regardless of the medium of communication through which it was conveyed. Like Farley, some scholars argue that the voters are not fools, and are not that easily manipulated by political images, televised or not. This argument directly contradicts the school of thought that argues television renders politics emptier and increasingly vapid, reducing deliberation over issues to mere spectacle. Politics, of course, has always been composed of both spectacle and substance, and politicians who fail to balance these elements are unlikely to be successful.

But for Farley, the medium was not the message, and he did not see a world in which political expertise would ever be displaced by performance. For him, politics always entailed an element of the performative, but was not reducible to it. Farley was no technological determinist, and he was probably correct in arguing "that Harry Byrd could defeat Cary Grant for the office of US Senator in Virginia and . . . Republican Senator Everett Dirksen would be hands down to defeat Paul Newman in Illinois." Those agreeing with Farley thus would not have attributed Ronald Reagan's victory over Jimmy Carter in 1980 to Reagan's experience as an actor, but to his superior organization, his clearer message, his more charismatic personality, and his political acumen. Similarly, they could explain Barack Obama's defeats of John McCain and Mitt Romney by noting his organizational capacities as well as his rhetorical abilities. Television has increased the importance of candidate performances, but performance alone is not determinative. We trust political rhetoric to the extent that we trust voters to evaluate it. Those evaluations have to be made differently in every different political and technological context.

Political structures are legitimated by rhetoric, and they influence the context and thus the practice of rhetoric as well. The McGovern-Fraser campaign reforms following the 1968 presidential election, for instance, mattered at least as much as television in creating a new kind of audience for presidents, and thus changed the ways presidents communicated with that audience. Those reforms, by mandating equal representation at party conventions, meant that the easiest way for states to comply with that mandate was to eliminate state party conventions and move to a system of primary elections. This eroded the power of party elites in deciding presidential nominees and meant that political success depended not on party loyalty so much as personal appeal. Presidents in fact now not only poll more often, but poll for personality and personal appeal as well as for policy. Personal politics, then, are facilitated both by the mass media and by the political system. These changes have their roots in the practices begun by FDR, and when coupled with other institutional changes such as the growth of the executive branch and the administrative bureaucracy, they have affected the role of the president in the national government and altered the president's relationship with the mass public as well.

Roosevelt thus began a sea change in American politics, in which domestically, significant political power moved from the states and localities to the federal government, and within that government, from Congress to the executive branch.

Internationally, the United States took on an increased role, displacing the empires of Europe as the dominant political and military force and contending with the USSR for international hegemony. This contest also invested the president with increased political responsibility, as he became the "leader of the free world." These changes added a different kind of authority to the institution. It is notable, for example, that John Kennedy's inaugural address specifically included an international audience. Prior to that moment, inaugurals were domestically oriented. Presidents had always spoken for the nation. They now spoke for and represented an important international constituency as well, a move that added both responsibility and increased the office's capacity to act in the international realm.

John Kennedy was, in some ways, the first television president, and both Lyndon Johnson and Richard Nixon, who began their political careers in a context dominated by organizational politics, fared less well in one dominated by electronic media. Reagan's inaugural, of course, was the first to include panoramic views of the Capitol as part of the coverage. It certainly did not hurt his public image for his administration to be publicly connected to the various symbols of the nation's past and patriotic present. That administration is thought of as marking the moment when the visuals required by television melded with the politics of the presidency. We may see in the Obama administration a similar moment with social media. But while media forms and formats affect the everyday practices of the presidency in different ways, the underlying logic of presidential communication remains the same. Presidential rhetoric, whether directed at members of other institutions, the mass public, or a varying combination of both, helps create and maintain institutional capacities required for governance. Rhetorical failures will equate to political failures, regardless of the medium of communication, as presidents as different as Herbert Hoover and Jimmy Carter illustrate. Getting the rhetoric wrong will almost always create obstacles for presidents. Unfortunately for presidents, getting the rhetoric right facilitates but does not guarantee political success. But the fact that rhetoric has limits does not mean that it should be avoided.

Like all political resources, rhetoric must be understood and wielded correctly if its benefits are going to be available.

Presidential candidates essentially talk their way into office in the course of campaigns. It is no surprise that presidents seem to think talking alone can solve some of their problems once in office. But it is not nearly that simple. Communicative ability has always been critical to the ways in which presidents govern. That communication has always required some understanding of the ways in which the media can further the president's agenda.

Mediated Presidential Rhetoric

There is good evidence that presidents do not have the power to command, either in Congress or among the mass public, and that their ability to use what Theodore Roosevelt famously referred to as the "bully pulpit" is of limited use in persuading people to take a specific stand on narrowly defined policy issues. But there is another way to understand the role of rhetoric, allowing for the power of presidents to set definitions, to associate certain policies with foundational American values and separate other policies from those values, and to create, maintain, and expand the institutional capacities of the office. Presidents do not directly control public opinion. They can, however, influence it in ways that are not always direct or clearly demonstrable.

Despite the fact that presidential capacities to control public opinion are limited, presidents and the media continue to act as if presidential communication is not only important, but even determinative. This means that regardless of its actual efficacy in terms of short-term, measurable change in public opinion, when presidents speak, the media pay significant attention. Coverage of specifically rhetorical events like inaugurals, State of the Union Addresses, and other major policy speeches remains high even as media coverage of the government and the president in general decrease. These moments continue to generate significant speculation prior to the speech, significant coverage of the speech, and significant commentary after the speech. They thus provide opportunities when the president, her

agenda, and her plans for legislating that agenda dominate the
nation's political news.

We know, for instance, that the issues presidents focus
on in their State of the Union Addresses receive more attention
from the media that those they ignore. As Obama's staff put
it in a tweet during a presidential visit to General Electric in
January 2014, "We're here because you're doing really good
stuff that everyone else needs to pay attention to." Like Obama,
all presidents understand that what they say and do receives a
disproportionate amount of attention. They can use this, as Obama
did at General Electric, to highlight events, people, and practices.
Sometimes this is purposeful; presidents can encourage physical
fitness by bike riding and jogging, as George W. Bush did. Their
hobbies and preferences translate into national trends—sales
at McDonald's reportedly went up as a result to Bill Clinton's
well-known predilection for Big Macs, and broccoli growers felt
the effects when George H. W. Bush's distaste for the vegetable
made national news.

Intentionally or not, presidents have an effect on the
national agenda. Like the media, they cannot tell the public
what to think, but they can help the public decide what to think
about, a process by which presidential agendas influence those
of the media and the mass public, and are in turn influenced by
the media and public agendas. Agenda setting is stratified and
presidential frames can dominate, but cannot control that process.
They can draw attention to issues by speaking, by hosting events
at the White House, through proclamations, and through other
ceremonial and policy initiatives. The very act of directing public
attention is important. Whether it results in immediate policy or
opinion change is much more debatable.

Presidential influence isn't confined to agenda setting,
however. Presidents also have a role in framing issues—affect-
ing not only what issues get discussed in the media but also the
terms through which they will be understood. Partisan debate, for
instance, is often a debate over which frame for an issue is the
most appropriate: are US actions abroad risking "blood for oil"
or "promoting democracy"? Is extending unemployment benefits

required by the social contract or an abrogation of it? Deciding the frame can influence both public opinion and congressional and administrative action. Frames also involve emotional valences—policy choices are subject both to appeals to good reasons and to the attachments associated with those reasons.

Presidents, then, by communicating on issues in particular ways, can influence much more than short-term public opinion. They can hope to influence the terms through which a policy is debated and the judgments that the public arrives at concerning the best response to those policies. They undoubtedly have more influence over foreign policy choices than they do regarding domestic policy—they face less competition and have a greater level of information than potential opponents.

Presidents do better at dominating the agenda when there is less competition. If a president wants to make education the highest national priority, for instance, she is likely to have more success if unemployment is low and the nation is not at war. In addition, presidents are better able to convey their message when they face less opposition and when their definition of events resonates with media and public perceptions. Presidents may not be successful in attempts to change public opinion, but they can certainly capitalize on it. To do so effectively, it helps to have a clear and consistent message, and to convey that message through as many outlets as possible. Ronald Reagan was an innovator in this regard. He and his staff were famous for their ability to influence media coverage, and they did so by choosing a "theme of the day," which was communicated from the White House, the departments and agencies, the president's staff, and, when appropriate, the president himself. This meant that reporters would either have to cover the White House's preferred story or go against the grain and find another story with little or no help from official sources. The system wasn't perfect, but it was thought to have given the Reagan team unprecedented influence over the media agenda.

This requires a great deal of discipline, and few administrations can manage it consistently, but it is an indication of the kind of power presidents seek and sometimes achieve. Influencing the media agenda is widely considered to be more difficult in the contemporary context, because the media are less overtly hierarchical, more fragmented, more interested in sensational stories than in-depth coverage, and thus more superficial. The "news hole" has expanded as well, and there is a constant need for "news," which means that "feeding the beast," has become more onerous. Politics has become, to some scholars' dismay, more focused on celebrity—ever since Bill Clinton appeared on *The Arsenio Hall Show*, late night talk shows have become as important a venue for presidential image building as the Sunday morning political shows, and now that Barack Obama has been on *The View* and *Between Two Ferns*, afternoon shows may well become important venues as well. These appearances can help solidify a president's image, for better or worse. But presidential participation in popular culture is not new. To use just a few examples, Lincoln's image circulated widely, and served a variety of agendas. Franklin D. Roosevelt's dog Fala was chair dog of a fundraising effort for the embattled British Isles and was later made an honorary private in the army as a result of a donation made on his behalf. Richard Nixon appeared on *Laugh-In,* and Gerald Ford introduced his press secretary, Ron Nessen, on *Saturday Night Live,* reversing the normal protocol of having the press secretary introduce the president. Presidents have sought political leverage through formal and informal, controlled and uncontrolled, participation in popular culture. Sometimes they have found it.

Thus, despite the evolving media environment, two things are worth noting here. First, presidents continue to have some advantages potential opponents lack. There may be more "noise" out there, and presidents may face more competition for public attention, but they still occupy an office of enormous power, and the media and the public will be attentive to how that power is articulated and used. Stories about the president continue to lead the national news, even if the audience for that news is shrinking. The president may have a smaller place on an increasingly large national stage, but the spotlight remains on him.

Second, the rhetorical task remains the same whether the media are hierarchical and monolithic or democratized and fragmented. A president's rhetorical agenda must be clear; it must be consistent with his public image and partisan affiliations; it must be uniform across the administration; and it should be conveyed through a workable narrative. In this media environment, as in the past, if the messages coming out of the White House are contradictory, confused, or inconsistent, the story will be about the contradictions, confusions, and inconsistencies, not about the substance of the policy under consideration. Presidents can't now, and probably never could, dependably "win the news cycle," but they can certainly guarantee that they will lose it if they get the rhetoric wrong. Getting the rhetoric right, though, depends largely on their ability to manage their relationship with both their audience inside the Beltway and their national audience.

The Changing American Polity

Contemporary presidents face a large, diverse, and often fractious polity, currently mobilized along sharply divided partisan lines and apparently willing to agree on little except their anger with and alienation from their national government. Because of the rise of presidential governance since the 1930s and the accompanying increase in policy responsibility centered in the executive branch, the president, rather than Congress, is expected to exercise the majority of political leadership. During the 2013 budget crisis, for example, House Speaker John Boehner (R-OH) insisted in a *USA Today* Op-Ed that "This is part of a larger pattern: the president's scorched-Earth policy of refusing to negotiate in bipartisan way on his health care law, current government funding, or the debt limit." While indicating the level of partisan bickering that characterized the discourse surrounding the government shutdown, this quotation also reveals the extent to which even members of the congressional leadership look to the White House for policy leadership, for coalition building, and for managing at least some of the details of the legislative process. Sometimes, of course, as in this case, the presidency also serves Congress as a convenient scapegoat (the reverse is often true as well: presidents don't hesitate to scapegoat Congress). Denizens of both institutions design, facilitate, and administer elements of national legislation, but because the president has the higher national profile, the focus of attention goes first to the White House.

Presidents still can—and still do—call private meetings and engage in personal negotiations with members of Congress. These meetings are also the subject of tweets by all participants and their staffs, who then post commentary on their Facebook pages as well as delivering it in person and on talk shows. This is not to imply that there are no secrets in the White House or Congress. But it is to argue that important legislation is carried out very much in the public eye.

Several points are worth noting here. First, while politicians in previous eras did not have instant access to their constituents, and they had fewer outlets through which they could express their views, it is also true that major pieces of legislation have always been the subject of public attention. For example, the "Great Debate" over the extent and nature of American neutrality raged in Congress, on the radio, and in the nation's newspapers throughout the 1930s. Films like *Mrs. Miniver* and *Sergeant York*, novels like Sinclair Lewis's *It Can't Happen Here*, and Edward R. Murrow's broadcasts from London contributed to public attention and public understanding of the war in Europe and its stakes for the United States as much as the columns by journalists like Dorothy Thompson and the news coverage of the congressional debates. Similarly, debates over civil rights, women's rights, abortion, gays in the military, and same-sex marriage are contested in and outside of the legislative arena and at local, state, and federal levels. They are debated, discussed, and framed in the various media associated with popular culture. So while it is easy, it is probably also unhelpful to overstate the changes in public access to political processes and to attribute that access to the fact of new media alone.

Second, when we argue that the presidency is more visible than ever before, it must be remembered that it is increasingly visible only to a fairly small percentage of the population. While every person who stops by the local grocery store may see tabloid headlines analyzing the state of the Obama marriage, relatively few Americans pay significant attention to government on a day-to-day or even a week-to-week basis. According to the nonpartisan Pew Research Center, for instance, in early 2013, 76 percent of respondents were "especially looking forward to" the Academy Awards; only 49 percent felt the same way about the upcoming midterm elections. Given the historically low approval Americans feel toward Congress, even this level of anticipation may reflect eagerness to dispense with incumbents rather than to join in a spirited and informed debate over the issues. Whatever the reason, as a percentage of the American population, few Americans are aware of, follow with any dedication, or have strong positive attachments to, our shared national government. So the problem for presidents is less about the degree of public scrutiny they face and more about getting any sustained public attention at all. And this has always been their major hurdle.

Third, the Americans who are paying attention have specific characteristics. Like primary voters, they are more likely to be white and well-educated than average citizens. They are also more likely to have strongly partisan views. This means that the "public opinion" most visible to politicians, whether it comes in the form of polls, editorials, letters, emails, or social media posts, is unlikely to represent "the public" at all. Presidents are attentive to public opinion and increasingly rely on polls to determine its contours. But their understanding of the public and its opinions is limited.

There are also important things to remember about the polity as a whole. The polity has expanded enormously since the inception of the modern presidency. When FDR championed "the forgotten man" and advocated broad national inclusion in policy making, he was speaking about a fairly narrow segment of Americans and to one that was even more restricted. Roosevelt did not, for example, challenge any aspects of Jim Crow, nor did he seek African American enfranchisement in the South. After passage of the Civil Rights and Voting Rights Acts, the passage of the Twenty-Sixth Amendment expanding the franchise to eighteen-year-olds, and once "identity politics" took hold in the national imagination, presidents and presidential candidates had to appeal to a more diverse electorate than had previously been the case, and had to do so in increasingly inclusive terms. The United State has never fit the model of the ideal democratic republic. Despite its progressive and even inclusive elements, the Constitution enshrined an exclusionary politics that has been amended over time. The contemporary system, of course, still rests on important exclusions and hierarchies. From a rhetorical point of view, one important question involves how our political language serves to justify and/or challenge the contradiction implicit in the promise of our founding documents and the practices that they instantiate.

The nation's increasing diversity on the one hand seems to indicate more national inclusion. On the other hand, it may also reinscribe a kind of elite-based politics. Certainly, increased enfranchisement indicates a broader, more democratic polity. This apparent diversification has made things more complicated for presidents and presidential candidates, for the time has long since passed when political elites could claim to speak for members of many groups without getting significant pushback from members of those groups. It is not sufficient to possess, for example, in Republican presidential candidate Mitt Romney's often ridiculed phrase, "binders full of women." Women (by no means a unified class of citizens) want and expect to receive a seat at the table.

Not only do outdated understandings of the role of previously underrepresented groups continue to linger, but we remain a very long way from anything that looks like political equality, despite the election of the nation's first African American president. Members of these groups are, as many scholars have noted, increasingly organized. But not all groups are equally able to organize. Those with greater resources—education, money, knowledge of the political system—are more likely to marshal systematic pressure on the government and are more likely to be successful in doing so than are their more impoverished neighbors. Some interests are unquestionably more powerful than others, more able to provide the donations that facilitate access, and more able to influence the tone and content of policy and policy rhetoric.

The audience for presidential rhetoric, then, is neither the narrowly restricted constituency that presidents like Thomas Jefferson faced, or even the broader and more inclusive polity of Franklin Roosevelt's day. The contemporary public is a complicated mix of mass and elite audiences, out of which every president must craft electoral and governing coalitions. These coalitions are rooted in political parties and their accompanying ideologies, but also find important expression through the individual, personal appeals of the specific president with a specific public image. Think, for example, of the "Reagan Democrats," who maintained loyalty to the Democratic Party and voted consistently for Reagan. Contemporary presidents, like their historical counterparts, must compete for the nation's attention with a variety of distractions, and must compete with other elites over the policy agenda. They must strategically engage members of the mass public, who can be understood variously in partisan, group, and individual terms. And they must do so in ways that alienate as few potential supporters as possible. Rhetoric is the vehicle through which all of these demands are met.

Conclusion: Navigating the New Terrain

The presidency is a kind of political prism, capturing, reflecting, and refracting elements of the national polity. Vagaries of public opinion, mediated versions of political reality, and individual personalities are all magnified and thus distorted by their contact with the executive institution. Presidents must recognize this distortion and also adapt to it, finding ways in the process to make that distortion work to their political advantage. In doing so, they must recognize the opportunities and dangers inherent in any form of mass communication.

It is easy to overstate the ways in which the contemporary media—characterized by its 24/7 news cycle, its often-hysterical immediate response to events, its fragmentation, its increasing reliance on social media platforms, and so on—have changed the nature of American politics. I am not arguing that these changes do not matter, but I am claiming that the underlying logics of presidential communication remain very much the same. Presidents have always had to find ways to communicate their understanding of the nation to others and have always had to seek an audience for their arguments. That audience has always primarily been other elites, but has also always included members of the mass public as well.

Presidents at least since FDR have all had a greater degree of political and policy responsibility than their predecessors, and a clearer representative function as well. They face an electorate that is at once more organized and increasingly inchoate; more diverse and still understood primarily through elites; less easily mobilized and more attentive to particularized claims in presidential rhetoric and also more insistent that they be included in it. But the demands of coalition building are pretty much what they have always been—presidents must find enough people who agree with them on enough things over time to authorize their administrations and policy preferences. The task is not a singular, one-time event, but a process that plays out over time, in specific situations. So it is to a consideration of those situations that we now turn.

Suggested Readings

Allen, Mark. *Why Romney Lost the 2012 Election.* Amazon: Kindle, 2012.

Azari, Julia, R. *Delivering the People's Message: The Changing Politics of the Presidential Mandate.* Ithaca, New York: Cornell University Press, 2014.

Balz, Dan. *Obama vs. Romney: 'The Take' on Election 2012.* Washington, DC: *The Washington Post,* 2013.

Becker, Lee B., and Tudor Vlad. "News Organizations and Routines." *The Handbook of Journalism Studies,* edited by Karrin Wahl-Jorgensen and Thomas Hanitzsch (Routledge, 2009): 59–72.

Bennett, Lance W. "The Burglar Alarm That Just Keeps Ringing: A Response to Zaller." *Political Communication* 20 (2003): 131–38.

Benoit, William L., and K. Kerby Anderson. "Blending Politics and Entertainment: Dan Quayle versus Murphy Brown." *Southern Journal of Communication* 62 (1996): 73–85.

Berry, Jeffrey M., and Clyde Wilcox, *The Interest Group Society.* 5th ed. New York: Pearson, 2008.

Burke, Kenneth. *A Rhetoric of Motives.* Berkeley: University of California Press, 1969.

Campbell, Karlyn Kohrs, and Kathleen Hall Jamieson. *Presidents Creating the Presidency: Deeds Done in Words.* Chicago: University of Chicago Press, 2008.

Cohen, Jeffrey E. "Presidential Rhetoric and the Public Agenda." *American Journal of Political Science* 39 (1995): 87–107.

Dalleck, Robert. *Ronald Reagan: The Politics of Symbolism.* Cambridge, MA: Harvard University Press, 1987.

Denton, Robert E. *The Primetime Presidency of Ronald Reagan: The Era of the Television Presidency.* New York: Praeger, 1988.

Drury, Jeffrey P. Mehlretter. *Speaking with the People's Voice: How Presidents Invoke Public Opinion.* College Station: Texas A&M University Press, 2014.

Edwards, George C. III. *On Deaf Ears.* New Haven: Yale University Press, 2003.

Edwards, George C. III. *The Strategic President: Persuasion and Opportunity in Presidential Leadership.* Princeton: Princeton University Press, 2009.

Edwards, George C. III, and B. Dan Wood. "Who Influences Whom? The President, Congress, and the Media." *American Political Science Review* 93 (1999): 237–344.

Eisinger, Robert M. *The Evolution of Presidential Polling.* New York: Cambridge University Press, 2003.

Engels, Jeremy. *Enemyship: Democracy and Counter-Revolution in the Early Republic.* East Lansing: Michigan State University Press, 2010.

Entman, Robert M. "Framing: toward Clarification of a Fractured Paradigm." *Journal of Communication* 43 (1993): 51–58.

Entman, Robert M. "Cascading Activation: Contesting the White House's Frame after 9/11," *Political Communication* 20 (2003): 413–32.

Fisher, Louis. *President and Congress: Power and Policy.* New York: Free Press, 1972.

Gilberg, Sheldon, Chaim Eyal, Maxwell McCombs, and David Nichols. "The State of the Union and the Press Agenda." *Journalism Quarterly* 57 (1980): 584–88.

Glavin, Daniel J. *Presidential Party Building: Dwight D. Eisenhower to George W. Bush.* Princeton: Princeton University Press, 2009.

Hart, Roderick P. *The Sound of Leadership: Presidential Communication in the Modern Age.* Chicago: University of Chicago Press, 1989.

Hart, Roderick P. *Seducing America: How Television Charms the Modern Voter.* Thousand Oaks, CA: Sage, 1998.

Hartnett, Stephen John. *Democratic Dissent and the Cultural Fictions of Antebellum America.* Champaign: University of Illinois Press, 2002.

Hertsgaard, Mark. *On Bended Knee: The Press and the Reagan Presidency.* New York: Farrar Strauss and Giroux, 1988.

Hill, Kim Quale. "The Policy Agenda of the President and the Mass Public: A Research Validation and Extension." *American Journal of Political Science* 42 (1998): 1328–34.

Hogan, Michael J. *Woodrow Wilson's Western Tour: Rhetoric, Public Opinion, and the League of Nations.* College Station: Texas A&M University Press, 2006.

Holbert, R. Lance. "A Typology for the Study of Entertainment Television and Politics." *American Behavioral Scientist* 49, no. 3 (2005): 436–53.

Iyengar, Shanto, and Donald R. Kinder, *News That Matters.* Chicago: University of Chicago Press, 1987.

Jacobs, Lawrence R., and Melanie Burns. "The Second Face of the Public Presidency: Presidential Polling and the Shift from Policy to Personality Polling." *Presidential Studies Quarterly* 34 (2004): 536–56.

Jamieson, Kathleen Hall. *Eloquence in an Electronic Age: The Transformation of Political Speechmaking.* New York: Oxford University Press, 1990.

LeLoup, Lance, and Steven Shull. *The President and Congress: Collaboration and Combat in National Policymaking.* 2nd ed. New York: Pearson, 2002.

McDonald, Ian R., and Regina G. Lawrence. "Filling the 24 × 7 News Hole: Television News Coverage Following September 11." *American Behavioral Scientist* 48 (2004): 327–40.

McCombs, Maxwell, and Donald E. Shaw. "The Agenda Setting Function of Mass Media." *Public Opinion Quarterly* 36 (1972): 176–87.

Mercieca, Jennifer R. *Founding Fictions.* Tuscaloosa: University of Alabama Press, 2012.

Milkis, Sidney M. *The President and the Parties: The Transformation of the American Party System since the New Deal.* New York: Oxford University Press, 1993.

Milkis, Sidney M. *Political Parties and Constitutional Government: Remaking American Democracy.* Baltimore: Johns Hopkins University Press, 1999.

Milkis, Sidney M., and Jerome M. Mileur, eds. *Progressivism and the New Democracy.* Amherst: University of Massachusetts Press, 1999.

Milkis, Sidney M., and Jerome M. Mileur, eds., *The New Deal and the Triumph of Liberalism.* Amherst: University of Massachusetts Press, 2002.

Norrander, Barbara. "Presidential Nomination Politics in the Post-Reform Era." *Political Research Quarterly* 49 (1996): 875–915.

Parenti, Michael. *Make-Believe Media: The Politics of Entertainment.* New York: St. Martin's Press, 1992.

Patterson, Thomas E., and Robert D. McClure, *The Unseeing Eye: The Myth of Television Power in National Elections.* New York: Putnam, 1976.

Peake, Jeffrey S. "Presidential Agenda Setting in Foreign Policy." *Political Research Quarterly* 54 (2002): 69–86.

Perelman, Chaim, and Lucie Olbrechts-Tyteca. *The New Rhetoric: A Treatise on Argumentation.* Notre Dame, IN: University of Notre Dame Press, 1989.

Piven, Frances Fox, and Richard Cloward. *Poor Peoples' Movements: Why They Succeed, How They Fail.* New York: Vintage, 1978.

Prior, Markus. "News vs. Entertainment: How Increasing Media Choice Widens Gaps in Political Knowledge and Turnout." *American Journal of Political Science* 49 (2005): 577–92.

Reinsch, J. Leonard. *Getting Elected; From Radio and Roosevelt to Television and Reagan.* 2nd ed. New York: Hippocrene, 1996.

Rogin, Michael. *Ronald Reagan: The Movie and Other Episodes in Political Demonology.* Berekely: University of California Press, 1988.

Rosentiel, Tom. *Strange Bedfellows: How Television and Presidential Candidates Change American Politics.* New York; Hyperion, 1992.

Rottinghaus, Brandon. *The Provisional Pulpit: Modern Presidential Leadership of Public Opinion.* College Station: Texas A&M University Press, 2010.

Schaefer, Todd M. "Persuading the Persuaders: Presidential Speeches and Editorial Opinion," *Political Communication* 14 (1997): 97–111.

Scheufele, Dietram A. "Agenda Setting, Priming and Framing Revisited: Another Look at Cognitive Effects of Political Communication." *Mass Communication and Society* 3 (2000): 297–316.

Schram, Martin. *The Great American Video Game: Presidential Politics in the Television Age.* New York: Morrow, 1987.

Seligman, Lester G., and Cary R. Covington. *The Coalitional Presidency.* Belmont, CA: Dorsey, 1989.

Shapiro, Robert Y. "Public Opinion, Elites, and Democracy," *Critical Review* 12 (1998): 501–28.

Southwell, Priscilla L. "A Backroom without the Smoke? Superdelegates and the 2008 Democratic Nomination Process." *Party Politics* 18 (2012): 267–83.

Spitzer, Robert J. *President and Congress: Executive Hegemony at the Crossroads of American Government.* New York: McGraw-Hill, 1993.

Smith, Ted J., and Michael J. Hogan. "Public Opinion and the Panama Canal Treaties of 1977." *Public Opinion Quarterly* 51 (1987): 5–30.

Strolovitch, Dara Z. *Affirmative Advocacy: Race, Class, and Gender in Interest Group Politics.* Chicago: University of Chicago Press, 2007.

Stuckey, Mary E. *Voting Deliberately: Creating Citizens, 1936.* University Park: Pennsylvania State University Press, 2015.

Thrush, Glenn, and Jonathan Martin. *The End of the Line: Romney vs. Obama: The 34 Days That Decided the Election.* New York: Random House, 2012.

Tulis, Jeffrey K. *The Rhetorical Presidency.* Princeton: Princeton University Press, 1987.

Wattenberg, Martin. *The Rise of Candidate-Centered Politics: Presidential Elections of the 1980s.* Cambridge, MA: Harvard University Press, 1991.

Wattenberg, Martin. "The Changing Presidential Media Environment." *Presidential Studies Quarterly* 34 (2004): 557–72.

Wood, B. Dan, and Jeffrey S. Peake. "The Dynamics of Foreign Policy Agenda Setting." *American Political Science Review* 92 (1998): 173–84.

Zaller, John, and Dennis Chiu. "Government's Little Helper: U.S. Press Coverage of Foreign Policy Crises, 1945–1991." *Political Communication* 13 (1996): 385–405.

Zarefsky, David. "Presidential Rhetoric and the Power of Definition." *Presidential Studies Quarterly* 34 (2004): 607–19.

═══ TWO ═══

Rhetoric from an Institutional
Perspective

As a young man, long before the office of the chief executive was invented, George Washington set down a set of *Rules of Civility & Decent Behavior in Company and Conversation.* These rules included instructions concerning the management of public sneezing, proper tones of voice, and the treatment of others, including a stricture against unwarranted flattery and notes on the proper conduct toward subordinates. In crafting these rules and endeavoring to live by them, Washington enacted his understanding that his public behavior would be considered an indication of his private character. By controlling that behavior, he sought to direct public perceptions of himself and his capacities. As an individual, he offered a model of leadership for a democratic polity.

Presidential rhetoric is tied to both the institution and the individual who occupies it. All presidents, for example, give inaugural and State of the Union addresses; they explain vetoes and travel the nation seeking support for their policy preferences. These occasions call for certain kinds of rhetoric. It is both possible and instructive to analyze presidential speeches as specific genres of discourse. But every president approaches generic tasks a little differently and accomplishes them in her or his own voice. Presidential speech is not purely generic and institutional. The public character of the person who speaks matters as much as the institutional platform from which the speech is given. Aristotle, discussing the forms of artistic proof, called this *ethos*, or what we might think of as public character. A person's ethos is not the same as her or his personality or private behavior. Ethos is what George Washington had in mind when he copied his rules of decorum. It is how we think of a public person: in previous eras we have thought of presidents as Old Hickory or Father Abraham. In our more cynical age, we think of presidents as Tricky Dick or Slick Willie. Ethos is what we mean when we think of a president like George W. Bush as inarticulate or Barack Obama as professorial. Ethos is what makes it possible for pundits, cartoonists, and citizens to summarize a president in a few words or images—Chevy Chase's rendition of a bumbling Gerald Ford called on the national belief that the office was too much for him by ignoring Ford's actual athleticism and David Letterman's "uh" count parodies Barack Obama's tendency toward pedantry. Ethos depends in part on audience—the ethos of a Bush or an Obama, for instance, has different emotional and cognitive valences for different audiences.

As these examples indicate, presidential ethos comprises but is also more than "image," because it involves a conflation of the institution with the individual. Individual presidents have specific kinds of attributes associated with them, a process that begins in their early political careers and solidifies during their campaigns. Woodrow Wilson, for example, was famously principled; Harry Truman was known to shoot from the hip and Dwight Eisenhower to be more measured; Franklin Roosevelt and Ronald Reagan were thought to be more thematically than detail oriented and Jimmy Carter and George H. W. Bush much the opposite. The elements of a president's public character are more or less set in the public mind by the time a president is elected. Those elements form an important part of the basis of public judgment of their administrations.

The institution has an ethos as well, and it interacts with that of the individual president. The delivery of their public pronouncements, like the content of those pronouncements, helps establish persons as presidents. Presidents are something of parental figures for the nation. They are supposed to be "strong," sometimes even "tough." They are expected to have certain kinds of deportment, specific manifestations of professionalism. The nation's shock at the Nixon Watergate tapes, for instance, was partially a response to the ethnic slurs, racial epithets, and strong language used in the Oval Office. The president's actions were reprehensible. The language through which he expressed himself was equally so, not least because the public wants its presidents to exemplify and call upon our "better angels," not give way to our less salubrious ones.

We want presidents to be able to interact with the "common people" and at the same time to be uncommon themselves. Jimmy Carter, for example, is widely considered to have tried to restore a more humble touch to the office after the problems associated with the "imperial presidency." He had some initial success with these efforts, too. His decision to walk to the White House following his inauguration, for instance, was warmly received by both the press and the public. But these efforts were also sometimes seen as stage managed rather than authentic, and his decision to speak to the nation wearing a cardigan seated before a fire was more ridiculed than admired. Ronald Reagan, on the other hand, was able to look as comfortable—and thus also as presidential—chopping wood at his ranch as wearing a tuxedo at state dinners. Neither the occasion nor the outfit alone can make a president look "presidential," however. Instead, the ease with which presidents adapt to various outfits and various occasions mark them as authentically at home in the executive mansion and among the nation's citizenry.

These examples illustrate the importance of individual personality and history and the central role of authenticity in the unreal world of the executive office. Reagan and George W. Bush could look presidential chopping wood because that activity came naturally to them. Neither Barack Obama nor George H. W. Bush would have enjoyed the same reception had either of them suddenly grabbed an axe. The presidency is an expansive institution, and it is possible to appear presidential by accenting one's intellectual capacities (Hoover, Kennedy, Clinton, and Obama), physicality (Theodore Roosevelt), trustworthiness (Eisenhower, Carter), candor (Truman), legislative ability (Johnson, Nixon), or political principles

(Wilson, Reagan). Other possibilities, of course, exist. But what a president cannot do is to abrogate the dignity of the office or appear to be uncomfortable in it, as Lyndon Johnson and Jimmy Carter too often seemed. Equally important is the appearance of consistency. Presidents must act in ways that resonate not only with the history of the institution but with their own public history as well. A president who has built her political career on being a military hawk and once in office advocates dramatic cuts in the defense budget must do some explaining. This doesn't mean presidents can never change their minds. It does mean that if they act in ways that make it seem as if there is no authentic self that animates their political decisions, the public will have difficulty trusting them.

Every public image provides both resources and obstacles. Richard Nixon, for instance, offered himself to the nation in 1968 as a "law and order" candidate, and the sense of stability thus offered was appealing to many citizens amid the turmoil of the 1968 campaign. It was particularly galling, then, that he and his aides broke the law in the name of maintaining order. Bill Clinton, on the other hand, survived the Lewinsky scandal in part because his sexual proclivities were largely known to the public and were part of his public persona. He built his appeal to the nation based on his policy ability rather than on his personal virtue. Policy failure would have been more difficult for him to manage than charges of financial maneuvering or sexual dalliance, both of which were at least implied by his reputation as "Slick Willie." It thus made perfect sense that his appeal to put the scandal behind him and "get back to work for the American people" resonated with supporters. In the same way, cold warrior Ronald Reagan was both deeply wounded by the perception that he had traded "arms for hostages" and able to recover from the scandal by relying on his reputation for being less than attentive to policy details. Scandal is often the result of a slippage between a president's perceived public character and public expectations and her or his actual activities. Presidents thus do well to rely on other aspects of that character in trying to recover.

Presidents collectively act the part of "president," and do so from some "authentic" core of individual character. The person interacts with the institution. This chapter explores the implications of that confluence for presidential rhetoric, beginning with the institutional resources available to presidents, including the organizational structures in the White House, speech writers, and surrogates. I then take up the individual side of the equation, focusing on the ways presidents can help create and maintain trust among the mass public. I conclude with a discussion of what it means to be "authentic" given the confines of the contemporary presidency.

Institutional Resources

Like all institutions, the executive office has resources embedded within it. While some scholars argue that the office has become more "rhetorical" over time, and especially because of the presidencies of Wilson and both Roosevelts, it has also become more connected to the president's relationship with the mass public rather than with Congress. While the issue of whether the presidency has come to rely more on rhetoric or not has, I think, been settled in favor of the negative, that isn't really the main point. As I understand them, the original critics of the "rhetorical presidency" argued that the combination of the media, election laws, and the ways in which we thought about presidential leadership led to a disruption of the constitutional order. That disruption did at least two things. It increased the amount of power accorded the president, and it premised that power on the president's relationship with the public rather than the parties. Both of these changes had the further consequence of skewing the political system. Presidents engaged in mass persuasion more than in institutionally based consultation, and as they became unmoored from the constraints of party organizations, they also lost the organizational capacities available only from parties.

In response, presidents began to develop their own campaign and governing organizations, deepening and thickening the executive bureaucracy in the process. As that bureaucracy grew, the parts of it dedicated to communication grew as well. FDR, for example, increased the number of staffers dedicated to news management by a huge margin. More recently, presidents have continued to woo the media in a variety of ways, some more successful than others. But the heart of that endeavor isn't personal charm; it's organizational skill. Here, I focus on three elements of that organization: the White House Office of Communications (WHOC), the speechwriting staff, and presidential surrogates.

The White House Office of Communications

In 1979, besieged by an energy crisis, the Hostage Crisis, and a general perception that the job might be too much for him, Jimmy Carter went canoeing in his home state of Georgia. While on the water, he encountered a "swamp rabbit," which swam toward his canoe with bared teeth. Carter responded by swiping at the rabbit with his paddle. An odd, but not nationally significant story, it was nonetheless captured on video by the accompanying press corps. The story might still have died, except that Carter's press secretary, Jody Powell, happened to mention it to AP correspondent Brooks Jackson. The story, capturing as it did the president attempting to protect himself from an animal generally considered harmless, and having minimal success doing so, seemed to capture the growing national understanding of the president and his administration. At least partly because it fit so well into the media narratives of the Carter administration, the "killer rabbit" story dominated headlines for about a week, miring the administration in a media nightmare and forcing it onto the defensive. Even worse, it did so on terms that rendered the president laughable. This story tells us a number of things about the media, the presidency, and the role of the WHOC in managing that relationship.

Because of the often-noted media obsession with conflict and drama, any appearance of disunity or disagreement inside the White House will make news, and it will not be the kind of news that favors the administration. This creates a problem for the president, because all good administrations require airing differences and discussing options, but the fact of such discussion can be covered as a symptom of disaffection and disorganization.

The job of managing the news belongs to the WHOC. Part of the president's personal staff, the WHOC runs polls, manages press relations (and attempts to manage the press as well), and endeavors to ensure that the messages coming from the various White House offices, the departments and agencies, and their collective staff, are consistent with the administration's agenda.

There is no question that the media and the presidency have grown together. The social power of the one has increased alongside the political power of the other. Both institutions, however, require at least the appearance of tension, which sometimes erupts into real conflict. If the relationship is best described, in media scholar Ithiel de Sola Poole's words, as "a bad marriage," there is no doubt that the WHOC is the marriage counselor. The WHOC staff work for the president, but must also work with the media. They try to put the president's spin on the news but must recognize the limits of that effort. Presidents can do a great deal to help the WHOC by being clear in their priorities, consistent in their arguments, and open to the input of those whose job it is to convey both the priorities and the arguments to the public.

The WHOC houses the press secretary, who is the president's most frequent and most direct link to the media. The press secretary must be able to accommodate the needs and demands of a competitive and often disgruntled press corps while also working to minimize the animosity natural to the media/ presidential relationship. A president who does not trust or who fails to fully inform her press secretary of ongoing events risks alienating the media who are likewise shut out of the policy process. Press secretaries have important managerial and symbolic roles. They literally speak for the president in her absence. They provide the media—and thus the public—with explicit information about policy and implicit information about how the administration does its business. So, for example, when Ford's press secretary Gerald Terhorst resigned in protest over Ford's decision to pardon Richard Nixon, that act influenced the national interpretation of the pardon.

Press secretaries are important buffers between the media and the president. According to one story, Eisenhower once asked his press secretary, Jim Haggerty, to make an announcement he knew would be unpopular with the press corps. Haggerty demurred, saying, "I can't, Mr. President. If I go out there and say that, they'll murder me." The president is said to have replied, "Better you than me, my boy," while shoving the hapless Haggerty out onto the stage. Eisenhower understood the value of having someone deliver bad news for him. Like most presidents, he did not always get the kind of coverage he wanted, but again like most presidents, he generally got the kind of coverage his organization facilitated.

Presidents should never underestimate the power of the media. As fragmented, fractured, and financially troubled as the industry is, it remains the single most important conduit of information from the president to the people and from the people, in the form of media questions, to the administration. Members of the media are adept at translating their opinions of White House operations to the public, even when the norms of objectivity and balance prevent them from doing so directly. They do so by the choice of stories and amount of coverage. A media corps that trusts the White House will be more likely to give it the benefit of the doubt. One that feels "managed" will be less likely to do so. The media can convey their opinions of a president's honesty, competence, and ability through vignettes, visuals, and "human interest stories." They see the president and her administration through the lens of the WHOC, and its organization and the abilities of those who work there can determine much about media perceptions of the administration as a whole. That office speaks for the administration and, when it does its job well, speaks clearly in the president's voice.

Speech Writers and the Presidential Voice

Presidents speak far more often and to a much wider set of audiences than ever before. In 1936 Franklin Roosevelt, running for reelection, gave roughly 60 speeches. In 2012 Barack Obama, also running for reelection, gave over 600. In both cases, many of these speeches were repetitions. Good campaigners, both presidents understood the value of thematically driven and consistent public speech. But someone had to write the words they spoke and it was not the presidents themselves. Good presidential communicators such as Roosevelt, Reagan, and Eisenhower paid attention to their rhetoric and often edited their speeches carefully. Even ones who were less adept or less interested, such as George H. W. Bush and Jimmy Carter, spent time on major addresses. Good editing, whether at the president's hand or that of an aide, ensures that the content is consistent with administrative policy. It also ensures that it is conveyed in the president's voice.

It is possible to write speeches that are more eloquent than the person giving them, that differ in tone from a person's natural way of speaking. These speeches often read well but are less clear when heard. George H. W. Bush, for instance, famously mangled many of his more high-flown texts and grew to loathe the demands for eloquence, and he developed real problems with what he called "the vision thing." Presidents, even those more comfortable with public communication than the first Bush, will rarely be at ease when delivering alien words and phrases, however well they are crafted, and that discomfort can come across to audiences as speech that is staged, fake, inauthentic. Speechwriters cannot write in the presidential voice if they do not have the opportunity to hear that voice. The best speeches are written by those who know the president's views and can translate them into the president's idiom. Some presidents have had fairly close relationships with their speechwriters; John Kennedy and Theodore Sorenson, for example, had a famous collaboration. But a close relationship isn't required. Peggy Noonan, who authored some of Ronald Reagan's most famous speeches, including the *Challenger* Address and the speech commemorating D-Day at Normandy, had very little access to the president himself. What she did have was an ear for his distinctive style and extensive files on his decades of remarkably consistent public speech.

Like the argument that television has rendered candidates somehow less authentic, the presence of speechwriters troubles those who argue that a president's words are somehow only "real" if she writes as well as delivers them. Speechwriters themselves underline the idea that their job is to help chief executives articulate their preferences, not to influence those preferences. This is something of a canard, because how one expresses ideas must always influence the ideas themselves, and the metaphors through which policies are conveyed influences the ways in which they are received and enacted. To address income inequality by declaring a "War on Poverty" is to accept the entailments of that metaphor—wars have enemies, they involve sacrifice, and so on. Language is not neutral. Like media frames, presidential language influences not just what we consider politically important but how we understand those things that are politically important. In helping to determine language, then, speechwriters inevitably influence policy. Content cannot be separated from form.

Though influencing policy, speechwriters do not neces-sarily therefore determine policy. Speechwriters can function as policy aides, but their words are usually carefully vetted. Journalist Sam Donaldson, writing during the 1980s, argued that the media's job was to put the president on the record. Presidential words, for him, were national policy, and it wasn't policy until the president said it was policy. Speechwriters influence policy by crafting the language through which it is understood, but it isn't policy until it has been accepted and articulated in some form by the president. By choosing to speak at some events and not others, by choosing to speak on some issues and not others, by choosing to speak in some words and not others, presidents themselves make the choices that matter. Sam Donaldson's view notwithstanding, those words do not necessarily have to come out of the president's mouth. Presidential rhetoric can usefully be understood as institutional as well as individual.

Surrogates

As often as presidents speak, they cannot speak to every constituency about every issue, and while they "go public" increasingly often, the demand for presidential attention grows even faster than their ability to accommodate it. Because presi-dential appearances garner so much attention, presidents may not always find it expedient to attend some events or speak on some issue themselves. For any number of reasons, then, presidents employ surrogates to take some of the rhetorical pressure off the chief executive.

The most important official surrogate is undoubtedly the vice-president. Lacking a specific portfolio, vice presidents can be used in a wide variety of ways. George H. W. Bush, for instance, who brought extensive foreign policy experience to the Reagan White House, often represented the president in international venues. He attended so many state funerals in that capacity that he joked about being the nation's official mourner. Vice-President Richard Nixon similarly served as the negative voice of the Eisenhower administration, going on the attack when necessary and allowing the president to remain above the political fray. Spiro Agnew occupied a similar position in the Nixon administration. Other vice-presidents have been valuable surrogates for their capacity to represent and speak to organized interests, regions, and states. Sending a vice-president to an event signals the White House takes that event and its audience seriously.

Ex-presidents can be important surrogates as well. Barack Obama, for instance, called Bill Clinton the "secretary of explaining stuff" following Clinton's performance at the 2012 Democratic National Convention. Ex-presidents, of whatever party, are the only people who genuinely understand the pressures of the office. Sitting presidents call upon them to validate their decisions, especially in foreign policy. When they can unite across partisan lines, as George H. W. Bush and Bill Clinton did in 2005 to promote relief for the victims and survivors of Hurricane Katrina, it sends a powerful message of national unity. Ex-presidents are more likely than vice-presidents to "go rogue," however, and speak their minds rather than reliably defending the current occupant of the White House, so they can be an especially tricky surrogate.

Members of the president's administration are generally more easily controlled than presidential predecessors. Cabinet officials often speak to their specific constituencies, which can be especially important as these events often earn very little national attention but the news surrounding them can travel widely to those interested in the specific issue area. This gives an administration an important set of choices—if it wants to trumpet an issue, the White House will be directly involved. If they want less news, announcements can be farmed out to cabinet secretaries or other policy aides. In a world of crowded media agendas and significant competition for the national news, this second communicative tier is useful for lower-level or more narrow policies that may not rise to the level of national interest.

Presidential spouses, who are presumed to have intimate relationships with the president, are in many ways ideally suited to speak with authority about the administration's preferences. First Ladies tread a number of very thin lines in a political position that has become increasingly complicated since the days when Eleanor Roosevelt traveled far and wide on her husband's behalf. They are criticized for doing too much and not enough; for being too subservient to their husbands and not subservient enough; for weighing in on policy and for failing to do so; for having careers and for giving them up. First Lady Nancy Reagan was considered to have too much influence over her husband. Similarly, Hillary Clinton was attacked for her interest in policy and for her tendency to try to infiltrate the West Wing while First Lady Laura Bush was sharply criticized for leaving governance to her spouse. First Ladies are powerful symbols of the contentions over the roles of women in our national political, social, and economic life, and they serve as barometers for the national lack of consensus over those roles. But when they speak for the administration and the president, they speak with great authority and can be important messengers.

White House communication, like all elements of administration, always eludes full control. The communication process, in fact, often seems to elude even the appearance of partial control as press secretaries obfuscate rather than clarify, speechwriters and staffers pick inappropriate locations or poor words, Cabinet members go "off message," ex-presidents make headlines with their policy views, and spouses exercise their own individuality. Throwaway phrases can become major markers, characterizing an entire administration. Franklin Roosevelt did not originally intend the "New Deal" to stand as the defining label of his presidency any more than George W. Bush foresaw the power of the phrase "the Axis of Evil." No White House has ever produced flawless policy or political communication, although some have done better than others. Those with a greater degree of success are those that have a greater degree of consensus about the overall aims of the White House and a greater degree of comfort with how the executive office is managed. Presidents can help themselves here by establishing clear lines of internal communication and by being attentive to the administrative requirements of their communication operations. They can also help themselves by nurturing their own relationship with the mass public.

Individual Resources

Presidents are individuals as well as office holders, and while as persons they have fewer resources at their command than they do as presidents, their own individuality is an important element in their political success. Public expectations of presidents are both complicated and contradictory. In order to be elected, candidates must fit into the mold of what the office requires. As presidents they face continual acclaim, criticism, and challenge. To be successful, presidents must enact the institutional role and must do so in ways that are congruent with their own personal ethos. There are dangers here. Lyndon Johnson, for instance, created problems for himself when he engaged in behavior that had attracted little attention when he was a senator, such as lifting his beagles by their ears and driving manically around his ranch in Texas. He had not changed, but his institutional position had, and he failed to accommodate himself to the changed expectations. The media, which once protected the private lives of presidents, no longer do so. Presidential miscues make front page news, and even President Carter, who had few personal missteps, was plagued by the seemingly endless capacity of his family to entertain the nation. More recently, Roger Clinton's exploits made national news, and even Barack Obama's Kenyan relatives (and alleged relatives) have had their share of media attention. Personal and familial foibles can come to represent the president's inability to control himself or his image, a perception that can be devastating to his public standing.

So the first personal resources are the president and the president's family. Presidential families have always been news, and that news has often been problematic. Theodore Roosevelt, for example, after being implored by a friend to minimize his oldest daughter's exploits, said, "I can either run the country or I can control Alice. I cannot possibly do both." This is probably the best attitude presidents can take toward their newsworthy relatives. Those relatives can never be controlled, and attempts to do so make more news and generate more controversy than simply letting them alone.

Presidential children are especially difficult because presidential parents want their children, especially their young children, to be as unharmed by media attention as possible while also realizing that portrayals of their families help humanize an otherwise remote public figure. In general, the mainstream media respect the rights of children to be left alone unless they perceive the White House as attempting to use them as political props. Once children are perceived as being used politically, the media are much less likely to keep their actions private. The older the children are, the more likely they are to be targets of news coverage. Thus, after the early troubles between the media and the Clintons concerning coverage of Chelsea, the media largely left her alone. The Bush twins, Barbara and Jenna, on the other hand, made news when they were cited for underage drinking in 2001. Both the illegality of their behavior and their ages made airing the story less controversial than the coverage of Chelsea had been. Obama's young children, Sasha and Malia, have been largely left alone, with coverage tending to emphasize their adorableness at ceremonial events.

By far, the president's greatest personal resource is himself. The first rule here is to conserve that resource. Presidents should be careful not to be overexposed, which leads the media both to expect to see him more often and to criticize the frequency with which they do see him. The question of which issues and venues merit presidential attention is important, for the presidential presence is the clearest available flag for administration priorities. So that presence needs to be used carefully. Presidents should be rehearsed, rehearsed again, and then again. Delivery is important, and the craft of speechmaking cannot be ignored. The rhetoric surrounding presidential appearances can be helpfully thought of in terms provided decades ago by congressional scholar Richard Fenno.

In one of his many works, Fenno studied the electoral and governing strategies of members of Congress as they communicated with citizens in their districts. He found that members were more likely to be reelected when they had established themselves as trustworthy. Fenno understood trust as being comprised of three elements, all of which are familiar to students of rhetoric: identification, empathy, and qualification. Successful congressional campaigners, Fenno found, established among their constituents the sense that the member had important values and beliefs in common with those constituents (identification), therefore shared their affective orientation toward important matters of public policy (empathy), and was competent to enact those preferences as legislation (qualification).

These elements are equally useful in understanding how presidents approach their communicative task. All presidents and presidential candidates seek to establish a sense of identification with their national audiences. This is displayed on the national level in vague celebratory nostrums about the nation. In smaller venues, it is why presidents don cowboy hats in Texas, eat hot dogs and pizza in New York and Chicago, dine on grits in the South, place bets on sporting events with political allies and rivals, show their appreciation for various businesses and unions, and, in short, do all manner of things that seem trivial if not absurd. In the larger scheme of things, they are neither trivial nor absurd. Presidents are performing a representative function, reminding members of these groups that they are valuable and valued parts of the nation. When presidents decide not to speak before a group such as the NAACP, it is understood as an overt act of exclusion.

So it is important for presidents to get their messages right. When Gerald Ford, visiting the Southwest, tried to eat a tamale without removing the corn husk wrapping, when Barry Goldwater ordered a kosher hot dog and a glass of milk when campaigning in New York, it was pretty clear that their efforts at identification failed.

Even if a president has nothing apparently in common with a constituency, it is still possible to forge affective bonds. Fenno called this empathy. Identification and empathy are closely related—so closely in fact, that for theorist Kenneth Burke, they are practically synonyms. Establishing empathy is establishing that the president and the public share an orientation toward matters of public concern. They accomplish this through overt acts of identification—think of the multiple times and places in which Bill Clinton declared that he felt the nation's pain—or more implicitly through association and dissociation. Harry Truman, for instance, positioned himself in 1948 against the "do-nothing" 75th Congress, associating himself with active and vigorous policy and dissociating himself from the more careful policymaking of the Republicans. Eisenhower, whose authority was associated with his military prowess in World War II, was the preeminent and unquestionable judge of military needs during his administration and the nation felt secure under his leadership—at least until John Kennedy promised a more youthful and vigorous approach to national defense. Empathy, like identification, is grounded in ethos, and it makes the implicit claim that because presidents are somehow akin to the people they govern, they both serve as surrogates for those people and will make appropriate policy decisions for them.

We trust people who are more like us. We may also trust people who, although different from us, understand and support us. But, Fenno argued, we will not elect people, however much they convince us of these things, if we don't see them as competent. Thus, presidents must be able to speak knowledgeably about policy. They do not need to be as famously wonkish as Bill Clinton or as professorial as Barack Obama to convey this competence. When talking to a broad national audience, the focus should be on the big picture. Presidents like Franklin Roosevelt and Ronald Reagan excelled at this while the more detail-oriented Jimmy Carter did not. The more restricted and narrowly focused the audience, the more important the details become—those audiences are likely to know more about the policy area than the president—but even then, being able to place that policy in the context of the administration's broader themes is critical to conveying competence.

Presidents like Herbert Hoover, Jimmy Carter, and George H. W. Bush failed to understand that their records did not speak for themselves. Presidents have increasingly become the center of mediated American political attention. In response, they have developed a large staff dedicated to communicating about the nation's policy. They have come to depend on press secretaries, speech writers, family members, and other surrogates to make their case to the nation's citizens. But if they fail to demonstrate that they willingly and appropriately represent the nation, share its values, and have its best interests at heart, and that they are capable of enacting policy to further those interests, those rhetorical failures will quickly translate into political failures.

Conclusion: "Authentic" Communication

Despite changes in the media and political environments of governance, the rhetorical imperatives haven't changed all that much since Aristotle. Contemporary political rhetoric has the same imperatives Richard Fenno noted in the late 1970s. Presidents who are rhetorically successful are those who are comfortable in their own skins and who can convey a sense of that comfort to the mass public. The second part of that claim is considerably more difficult to achieve than the first. To all appearances, for instance, both George H. W. Bush and Jimmy Carter were and are satisfied with themselves as human beings and also as presidents. But both of them considered public communication a distraction from the "real" elements of the job, and this undermined their ability to accomplish the tasks they considered central.

It may also be true that the most successful presidents are those whose particular skills are clearly conveyed over the prevailing forms of mass media. It helps if they are telegenic, but looking good on television is neither always necessary nor sufficient for political success. Good communication can mitigate a multitude of other weaknesses, but few political strengths can overcome the problems associated with poor communication. That communication must be organized in order to be successful. From the communications director and press secretary on down, the staff must know the president's priorities and must be consistent in how they talk about them. This is possible only if the president and her senior staff are themselves clear about those priorities. The critics of contemporary rhetoric are critical largely because they observe an absence of content in the rhetoric of too many political actors. Good political rhetoric must contain deliberative elements if it is to sustain democracy. Presidents have a good many chances to engage in that kind of rhetoric, and the next chapter treats both the rhetorical opportunities and dangers inherent in the executive office.

Suggested Reading

Anderson, Karrin Vasby, and Kristy Horn Sheeler. *Woman President: Confronting Postfeminist Political Culture*. College Station: Texas A&M University Press, 2013.

Anthony, Carl Sferrazza. *First Ladies: The Saga of the Presidents' Wives and Their Power*. New York: Morrow, 1991.

Arnold, Peri. *Making the Managerial Presidency: Comprehensive Reorganization Planning, 1905–1996*. Lawrence: University Press of Kansas, 1998.

Barber, James David. *The Presidential Character: Predicting Performance in the White House*. 2nd ed. Englewood Cliffs, NJ: Prentice Hall, 1977.

Benson, Thomas W. *Writing JFK: Presidential Rhetoric and the Press in the Bay of Pigs Crisis*. College Station: Texas A&M University Press, 2004.

Bucy, Erik P., and Maria Elizabeth Grabe. "Taking Television Seriously: A Sound and Image Bite Analysis of Presidential Campaign Coverage, 1992–2004." *Journal of Communication* 57 (2007): 652–75.

Burns, Lisa M. *First Ladies and the Fourth Estate: Press Framing of Presidential Wives*. DeKalb: Northern Illinois University Press, 2008.

Ceaser, James W., Glen E. Thurow, Jeffrey K. Tulis, and Joseph M. Besette. "The Rise of the Rhetorical Presidency." *Presidential Studies Quarterly* 11 (1981): 158–71.

Campbell, Karlyn Kohrs, and Kathleen Hall Jamieson. *Presidents Creating the Presidency: Deeds Done in Words*. Chicago: University of Chicago Press, 2008.

Campbell, Karlyn Kohrs Campbell, and Kathleen Hall Jamieson. "Inaugurating the Presidency," *Presidential Studies Quarterly* 15, no. 2 (1985): 394–411.

Caroli, Betty Boyd. *First Ladies*. New York: Oxford University Press, 2003.

Cohen, Jeffrey. *Going Local: Presidential Leadership in the Post-Broadcast Age*. Cambridge: Cambridge University Press, 2009.

Davis, Vincent, ed. *The Post-Imperial Presidency*. Piscataway, NJ: Transaction, 1980.

Donaldson, Sam. *Hold On, Mr. President!* New York: Random House, 1987.

Evans, Rowland, and Robert Novak. *Lyndon B. Johnson: The Exercise of Power*. New York: New American Library, 1966.

Edwards, Jason A. *Navigating the Post-Cold War World: President Clinton's Foreign Policy Rhetoric*. Lanham, MD: Rowman & Littlefield, 2008.

Fahnestock, Jeanne *Rhetorical Style: The Uses of Language in Persuasion*. New York: Oxford, 2011.

Fenno, Richard F. *Home Style: House Members in Their Districts*. Boston: Little, Brown, 1978.

Fisher, Walter R. "Rhetorical Fiction and the Presidency." *Quarterly Journal of Speech* 66 (1980): 119–26.

Grover, William F. *The President as Prisoner: A Structural Critique of the Carter and Reagan Years*. Albany: SUNY Press, 1989.

Heith, Diane J. "Staffing the White House Public Opinion Apparatus 1969–1988," *Public Opinion Quarterly* 62, no. 2 (1998): 165–89.

Ivie, Robert L., and Oscar Giner. "American Exceptionalism in a Democratic Idiom: Transacting the Mythos of Change in the 2008 Presidential Campaign." *Communication Studies* 60 (2009): 359–75.

Jamieson, Kathleen M. Hall. "Generic Constraints and the Rhetorical Situation." *Philosophy & Rhetoric* 6 (1973): 162–70.

Jamieson, Kathleen Hall, and Karlyn Kohrs Campbell. "Rhetorical Hybrids: Fusions of Generic Elements." *Quarterly Journal of Speech* 68 (1982): 146–57.

Kaufman, Burton I. *The Post Presidency from Washington to Clinton.* Lawrence: University Press of Kansas, 2012.

Kengor, Paul. *Wreath Layer or Policy Player: The Vice President's Role in Foreign Policy.* Lanham, MD: Lexington Books, 2000.

Kernell, Samuel. *Going Public: New Strategies of Presidential Leadership.* 4th ed. Washington, DC: CQ Press, 2006.

Kumar, Martha Joynt. "Communications Operations in the White House of President George W. Bush: Making News on His Terms." *Presidential Studies Quarterly* 33 (2003): 366–93.

Kumar, Martha Joynt. *Managing the President's Message: The White House Communications Operation.* Baltimore: Johns Hopkins University Press, 2007.

Hult, Karen M., and Charles E. Walcott. *Empowering the White House: Governing Under Nixon, Ford, and Carter.* Lawrence: University Press of Kansas, 2003.

Lim, Elvin T. "The Presidency and the Media: Two Faces of Democracy." In *The Presidency and the Political System,* 10th ed., edited by Michael Nelson, 258–71. Washington, DC: CQ Press, 2013.

Linsky, Martin. *Impact: How the Press Affects Federal Policymaking.* New York: WW Norton, 1986.

Maltese, John A. *Spin Control: The White House Office of Communications and the Management of Presidential News.* Charlotte: University of North Carolina Press, 1994.

Martin, Martha Anna. "Ideologues, Ideographs, and 'The Best Men': From Carter to Reagan." *Southern Speech Communication Journal* 49 (1983): 12–25.

Mayer, Jeremy D. "The Presidency and Image Management: Discipline in Pursuit of Illusion." *Presidential Studies Quarterly* 34 (2004): 620–31.

Medhurst, Martin J. "Religious Rhetoric and the Ethos of Democracy: A Case Study of the 2000 Presidential Campaign." *The Ethos of Rhetoric,* edited by Michael J. Hyde (University of South Carolina Press, 2004): 114–35.

Miroff, Bruce. "From 'Midcentury' to Fin-de-Siècle: The Exhaustion of the Presidential Image." *Rhetoric & Public Affairs* 1 (1998): 185–99.

Noonan, Peggy. *What I Saw at the Revolution: A Political Life in the Reagan Era.* New York: Random House, 1990.

O'Connor, Karen Bernadette Nye, and Laura Van Assendelft, "Wives in the White House: The Political Influence of First Ladies." *Presidential Studies Quarterly* 26 (1996): 835–53.

Parry-Giles, Shawn J., and Trevor Parry-Giles. "Gendered Politics and Presidential Image Construction: A Reassessment of the 'Feminine Style.'" *Communications Monographs* 63 (1996): 337–53.

Patterson, Thomas E. *Out of Order.* New York: Knopf, 1993.

Perelman, Chaim, and Lucie Olbrechts-Tyteca, *The New Rhetoric: A Treatise on Argumentation.* Notre Dame, IN: University of Notre Dame Press, [1969] 2000.

Regan, Don. *For the Record: From Wall Street to Washington.* New York: Harcourt, Brace, Jovanovich, 1988.

Reyes, G. Mitchell. "The Swift Boat Veterans for Truth, the Politics of Realism, and the Manipulation of Vietnam Remembrance in the 2004 Presidential Election." *Rhetoric & Public Affairs* 9 (2006): 571–600.

Ritter, Kurt, and Martin J. Medhurst, eds. *Presidential Speechwriting: From the New Deal to the Reagan Revolution and Beyond.* College Station: Texas A&M University Press, 2003.

Rojecki, Andrew. "Rhetorical Alchemy: American Exceptionalism and the War on Terror." *Political Communication* 25 (2008): 67–88.

Rottinghaus, Brandon. *The Provisional Pulpit: Modern Presidential Leadership of Public Opinion.* College Station: Texas A&M University Press, 2010.

Rudalevige, Andrew. *The New Imperial Presidency: Renewing Presidential Power after Watergate.* Ann Arbor: University of Michigan Press, 2005.

Scharrer, Erica, and Kim Bissell. "Overcoming Traditional Boundaries: The Role of Political Activity in Media Coverage of First Ladies." *Women & Politics* 21 (2000): 55–83.

Schlesinger, Arthur M. Jr. *The Imperial Presidency.* New York: Mariner Books, 2004.

Sigelman, Lee. "Presidential Inaugurals: The Modernization of a Genre." *Political Communication* 13 (1996): 81–92.

Smith, Craig Allen. "President Bush's Enthymeme of Evil: The Amalgamation of 9/11, Iraq, and Moral Values." *American Behavioral Scientist* 49 (2005): 32–47.

Smith, Craig R. *Confessions of a Presidential Speechwriter.* East Lansing: Michigan State University Press, 2014.

Stuckey, Mary E. *Strategic Failures in the Modern Presidency.* Cresskill, NY: Hampton Press, 1997.

Stuckey, Mary E. "Rethinking the Rhetorical Presidency." *Review of Communication* 10 (1): 38–52.

Tulis, Jeffrey K. *The Rhetorical Presidency.* Princeton: Princeton University Press, 1987.

Valenzano, Joseph M. III, and Jason A. Edwards. "Exceptionally Distinctive: President Obama's Complicated Articulation of American Exceptionalism." In *American Identity in the Age of Obama,* edited by Amilcar Antonio Bareto and Richard L. O'Bryant, 175–98. New York: Routledge, 2014.

Vatz, Richard E. "Public Opinion and Presidential Ethos." *Western Journal of Communication* 40 (1976): 196–206.

Vaughn, Juston S., and Lily J. Goren, eds. *Women and the White House: Gender, Popular Culture and Presidential Politics.* Lexington: University Press of Kentucky, 2012.

Walcott, Charles E., and Karen M. Hult. *Governing the White House: From Hoover through LBJ.* Lawrence: University Press of Kansas, 1995.

Washington, George. *George Washington's Rules of Civility & Decent Behavior in Company and Conversation.* Boston: Applewood Books, 1989.

Wertheimer, Molly Meijer, ed. *Leading Ladies of the White House: Communication Strategies of Notable Twentieth-Century First Ladies.* Lanham, MD: Rowman & Littlefield, 2005.

Zarefsky, David. *President Johnson's War on Poverty: Rhetoric and History.* Tuscaloosa: University of Alabama Press, 1986.

THREE

MANAGING RHETORICAL OPPORTUNITIES

During his 1982 State of the Union Address, Ronald Reagan did something no president had ever done before. Looking up to the balcony where First Lady Nancy Reagan and her guests sat, he said, "Just two weeks ago, in the midst of a terrible tragedy on the Potomac, we saw again the spirit of American heroism at its finest, the heroism of dedicated rescue workers saving crash victims from icy waters. And we saw the heroism of one of our young Government employees, Lenny Skutnik, who, when he saw a woman lose her grip on the helicopter line, dived into the water and dragged her to safety." The presence of Skutnik himself in the gallery made this moment unique. For the first time during a State of the Union Address, a president made use of a living example to underline an argument about the nature of American citizenship and American national identity. Those living examples at major addresses are now standard, and the discussion of who will be joining the First Lady and what her guests represent are now commonplace. So commonplace, in fact, that these guests are known among the Washington press corps as "Skutniks." Like the original Lenny Skutnik, all "Skutniks" are examples of presidential attempts to seize and capitalize on a rhetorical moment.

Political life is full of rhetorical opportunities. Talk is, after all, the medium through which politics is enacted. Critics of the rhetorical presidency often assume that the office has been—or is teetering on the brink of—being reduced to public performance, for rhetoric is indeed the bridge between the

43

presidency and the people. These scholars and pundits worry that relationship between the president and the mass public, pursued through increasingly familiar forms of speech, is one that pretends to intimacy but in reality is just spectacle. We see countless images of presidents and their families; we appear to have access to their lives "behind the scenes;" we may feel that we know them. But we do not actually have knowledge of their private selves. Even their public selves are available to us only through mediated formats.

We know that those formats are fragmented, with more and more outlets dedicated to increasingly narrow segments of a more highly partisan public. We know that there is enormous competition for public attention, and that even though the president has more command of the national stage than any other single political actor, her command is far from total and the stage is almost always shared. And we know that even once the public is paying attention, persuading them is a task of enormous complexity. This task is so difficult and complex, in fact, that some scholars, most prominently George C. Edwards. III, encourage presidents to spend significantly less of their time and energy on it. As should be clear by now, I disagree with that advice and argue that rhetoric, while probably largely ineffective as a tool of short term public opinion change on narrowly defined issues, is in fact useful to presidents in a variety of ways. If presidents seize and exploit the rhetorical opportunities inherent in their office, public speech can, in fact, contribute to political and policy success and institutional capacities for action.

This chapter therefore focuses on those rhetorical opportunities. First, I briefly discuss the ceremonial and deliberative opportunities inherent in the presidency. Then I discuss the episodic events that provide rhetorical and political resources for presidents, focusing on crisis, press conferences, and major policy addresses. I move from moments presidents can exploit to the avoidance of failure, and discuss rhetorical responses to gaffes and scandal. I conclude the chapter with a brief discussion of the integral relationship between presidential rhetoric and presidential politics.

Routinized Rhetoric

One theme of this book has been the extent to which presidents treat governing as synonymous with speaking. Undeniably, presidents speak increasingly often and to more kinds of audiences than they once did. This change is often attributed to the growth of mass media, and it is ironic that as the modes of communication available to convey presidential speech proliferate, the audiences for such speech diminish. Even if the actual viewing audience is relatively small compared to the overall population, major speeches still receive more sustained attention than almost any other political event. The reward for succeeding at such moments may be ephemeral, but the cost of failing to take advantage of such opportunities is clear. Presidents who miss rhetorical opportunities are diminishing the range of political opportunities available to them.

Presidents have a wide range of predictable opportunities like the State of the Union Address and the annual speech to the United Nations General Assembly. While all presidential speeches include both ceremonial and deliberative aspects, it can be useful to think of them separately because the expectations of the "merely" ceremonial differ from those associated with policy based speech. In ceremonial address, for example, audiences expect a certain amount of *pathos*, or appeals to emotion—these speeches tend to stress the importance of values without necessarily asking for action based on those values. Deliberative speeches, on the other hand, are expected to be grounded in *logos*, or reason, and tend to assume values and focus on action. This is, as we will see, a matter of degree, but attention to these expectations can make a speech more successful. Rhetoricians assume that speech is more likely to succeed when it is attentive to situation. They differ on the question of how much choice a speaker has in terms of responding to material conditions or creating them, and how much choice they exercise over the rhetoric itself—the extent to which they channel and create ideological language. Presidents both respond to and create political moments, and they channel as well as challenge specific national ideologies. In general, they do so in the service of their policy goals and in terms that will aggrandize the institutional power of their office.

Ceremonial Events

Without question, the inaugural receives more attention than any other ceremonial presidential address. Inaugurals, above all, are supposed to reveal something about the new administration. They rehearse the values that underlie that administration and offer insight into the president's view of national history and the contours of national identity. Of all forms of presidential speech, inaugurals are the closest to the purely ceremonial. They are not normally concerned with policy so much as the values that guide that policy. They tell the nation's story, from the perspective of the specific president, in a way that inevitably authorizes the administration to come. So when Dwight Eisenhower declared in 1953 that his inaugural marked a moment when "We are summoned by this honored and historic ceremony to witness more than the act of one citizen swearing his oath of service, in the presence of God. We are called as a people to give testimony in the sight of the world to our faith that the future shall belong to the free," he was asserting both the primacy of the Cold War and his approach to prosecuting it, an approach that depended on the mobilization of faith as much as military might. Similarly, Lyndon Johnson argued in his 1965 inaugural, "In a land of great wealth, families must not live in hopeless poverty. In a land rich in harvest, children just must not go hungry. In a land of healing miracles, neighbors must not suffer and die untended. In a great land of learning and scholars, young people must be taught to read and write." Those arguments did not defend policy specifically, but set out the values that would guide his policy preferences.

Inaugurals, however, are not the only moments when presidents get to underline the values that determine their political choices. Presidents spend a fair amount of time in the White House meeting with representatives of various groups and constituencies. These events occur so frequently that while they are in many respects episodic, it makes sense to think of them as routine. Presidents spend a great deal of time on these kinds of events. They greet Girl Scouts and members of winning sports teams. They welcome members of 4-H Clubs and the Model UN. They listen to Glee Clubs, marching bands and barbershop quartets. They invite scientists, entertainers, activists, and athletes to the White House. They offer toasts to visiting dignitaries. They profess amazement at the size of pumpkins, pardon turkeys, and engage in all manner of apparent silliness designed to make sure that they are seen as accessible to the public, dedicated to the middle class, enamored with our youth and elderly, proud of national traditions, respectful of various regions and religions, and in touch with the national culture. In some respects, these occasions are clearly a waste of presidential time. Certainly, there is apparently nothing here for those who think that the office ought to be the center of civic deliberation over specific policy proposals. Except that, when properly understood, they do in fact offer deliberative opportunities.

These occasions fall under the heading of *epideictic* rhetoric, or speeches of praise and blame. In choosing who to praise and what to blame, presidents can make very clear statements about their priorities and those of the nation. Ceremonial addresses, like inaugurals and eulogies, are the speeches most likely to have "eloquence" as part of the standard of judgment. When successful, these occasions offer the president the chance to make his case by relying on the representative value of average citizens. They allow the president to make her narrative of national history and the place of her administration within that history both personalized and compelling. The child who won the national spelling bee is a chance to stress the values of hard work and the importance of education; the entrepreneur who started a cupcake business, like the farmer who grew the largest pumpkin and the civic group who made important charitable contributions, have all risen to the level of presidential attention because they are ordinary people who have done something, or stood for something, or represent something the nation values or can be taught to value.

These moments are rarely publicized nationally, although generally there will be local attention given to them. They are so trivial that they occur almost invisibly except to those involved and to their local communities. But they are all chances to make the president's case, in person, to voters and, and through them, to those local communities, and to do so without engaging with their political opponents. They allow the president to connect individual stories with a larger narrative of the nation as a whole. These events are unlikely to change many minds on issues, but they offer the chance for the president to underline his programs, connect them to the values important to those citizens, and implicitly make the case for his leadership.

These events occur without the intervention of the opposition. No member of Congress, however much they may disdain the president, is likely to oppose the honoring of their constituents. Because these occasions are apparently lacking in policy content, deliberative argument is not mobilized in opposition. A president who honors the Teacher of the Year can use that opportunity to make an indirect case for her views on education, for the very indirection of the moment prevents argument about the merits of that case. No one rebuts an inaugural, and no one challenges a president who honors the accomplishments of citizens. Presidents, especially in what we are constantly told is a hyper partisan era, rarely get the opportunity to speak without being opposed. Ceremonial events provide a virtually unending series of such opportunities for presidents to make their policy case without going into the details of policy debate.

Speaking in foreign countries or to foreign dignitaries offers a similar set of rhetorical resources. These occasions are especially helpful to a president, for often politics continues to abate, if not stop entirely, at the water's edge, and foreign travel both engages public attention and generally works to the president's advantage in terms of public opinion. It is, of course, always better to avoid gaffes in such circumstances, but generally speaking, these are moments when presidents, acting as chief of state rather than as an explicitly "political" leader, have a chance to stand in the national spotlight without competition or significant internal criticism.

Presidents have the opportunity of giving a Farewell Address. Sometimes, their final State of the Union has elements of a farewell. In these addresses, presidents offer interpretations of their administrations and offer the criteria by which they hope those administrations will be judged. Like other kinds of ceremonial address, their opponents will differ with the content of the speech, but are unlikely to be ungracious enough to say so.

Because ceremonial events provide such a wealth of opportunity to offer their understanding of the nation to the public, presidents must give these opportunities the attention they deserve. Instead of treating such events as trivial or disconnected from the "real" job of president, presidents should take them as serious aspects of that job. Presidents, especially those who mistrust rhetoric or display little oratorical talent, tend to assume that these events are distractions from the job. Jimmy Carter and George H.W. Bush, for example, both tended to understand their office as a place where policy was made. The equally wonkish Bill Clinton understood that communicating that policy required sensitivity to its human components and consequences. Style is an important part of ceremonial address, which means that the president must be careful to both present the administration's ideas well and in her own vernacular. These events center on the mobilization of symbolic resources. Failure to take that task seriously can contribute to a rhetorically weak—and thus a politically weak—presidency.

Deliberative Events

The most obviously important of the deliberative opportunities is the State of the Union Address (SOU). No policy address gets as much sustained attention as this one, a fact that is all the more important because it is an extremely difficult speech to do well. Only one State of the Union, for example, FDR's 1941 "Four Freedoms" address, made the list of top 100 speeches of the twentieth century. Partly, the SOU is so difficult because it is the primary vehicle for administration policy; every cabinet department, agency, and interest has a stake in the speech and fights to get included in the text. They also fight to control the wording of the text, and this complicates the task of writing a speech that emphasizes the presidential voice and clearly speaks to administration themes.

Beginning with the Clinton administration in 1997, the speech has been streamed online as well as broadcast on television and radio. This increases the ease with which both domestic and international audiences can access the address. More importantly, it's a technology that allows the White House to "enhance" the address by adding all kinds of information supporting the president's case as it is being made. It also allows the public to interact with and recirculate that material as the speech progresses. White House staffers also strategically tweet during the speech, making it clear which ideas, policies, and word choices they want to highlight. Interactivity is not the same as civic engagement, of course, and the use of images may attract audiences and yet subvert congressional and public deliberation. But if the president intends to mobilize the administration's supporters rather than persuading opponents or encouraging deliberation and discussion, the tactic will remain appealing.

Speechwriter and scholar Craig R. Smith summarizes the elements of good deliberative address as outlined by Aristotle. Speakers, Smith notes, should gain audience attention and establish common ground. They should organize the argument for the policy in clear and easily understood terms and include elements that help the audience appreciate the consequences of the proposed action in memorable terms. We are likely to understand a "successful" policy address as one that convincingly makes the administration's case that a particular policy or set of policies is required, superior to its alternatives, and accurately reflects foundational national values. The key to making these addresses, then, lies in the connections between values and policies, generally conveyed through narratives that mobilize national history and mythology. This, of course, explains why presidents have continued to rely on the presence of specific individuals in the gallery. These "Skutniks," survivors of bombings and school shootings, teachers, fire fighters, soldiers, and activists, not only provide a visual element underscoring a president's theme and agenda, but also allowed for a connection between common citizens and the president, establishing a personal link between the chief executive and the nation.

The SOU should not be considered a stand-alone address, but the beginning of a policy discussion. If given early in the term, it can be helpful to think of the inaugural as setting out the values by which the president will be guided, the State of the Union as the expression of the policies that naturally stem from those values, and the Budget Message (which generally follows soon after the State of the Union) as the clearest statement of the ways in which the administration prioritizes those policies. If the White House understands its rhetoric this way, it can then decide how to organize the policy debates and legislative agenda that follow the State of the Union Address. One important vehicle for conveying the president's contribution to that debate is the weekly radio address.

Franklin D. Roosevelt famously used the radio as a vehicle for authorizing his leadership and promoting his policies. No other president made such good use of the radio until Ronald Reagan began the practice of delivering brief weekly talks. The advantage of these talks is that they earn little media attention. Presidents can talk to their own constituency, and can do so in an unfiltered way that generally doesn't create partisan debate. This means that presidents have an opportunity to make their message clear to their supporters—and to do so using language that can later serve as shorthand for their supporters while passing unnoticed by their detractors. Presidents can thus use the weekly radio address as a targeted method of "going public" on specific actions or pieces of legislation.

Many of these routinized modes of communication are easily taken for granted largely because they are routine. Presidents and their staffs give considerable attention to the rhetoric of inaugurals and State of the Union Addresses. It is easy to write off the resources these smaller occasions make available. Doing so is a mistake. The presidency is a public institution and to ignore the public aspects of the job is also to ignore its politics.

No president who fails to negotiate with Congress will be successful, but no president who fails to publicly lay out the broad themes of his administration or to connect his policy preferences to those themes is likely to have continuing success either.

Episodic Opportunities

Presidents speak at routine and predictable times. They can also create rhetorical opportunities. Many of these opportunities are policy-based, such as when they go on national or regional tours or visit specific sites in efforts to encourage and mobilize support for their policies. So they might arrange a visit to a factory to talk about jobs, for example. They give press conferences and they make statements following events of national import. Many of these moments feel trivial and if treated as "merely" symbolic, as "just rhetoric," opportunities to create and mobilize support for a president and potentially for a president's program can be lost. Similarly, ignoring the symbolism inherent in some locations can also be a mistake, as Ronald Reagan discovered when he visited Bitburg, Germany, in 1985. A moment he and his staff wanted to symbolize American and German friendship turned sour when it was discovered that the cemetery housed the bodies of former SS officers, and Reagan was charged with honoring Nazis and showing disrespect to the Jewish community. Reagan generally was more attentive to the symbolic associations of his actions, and generally had more success with his ceremonial address. Ceremonial events can be used to promote policy agendas and to legitimize presidential authority if presidents remember to make use of them and are attentive to the visual and other rhetorical accoutrements of the event.

Major events also increasingly call for presidential speech, whether that means sending good wishes to an Olympic team or responding to a national crisis. As presidents took more policy responsibility and a more central place on the national stage, they also became more integral to uniting the public in times of crisis. This often means military engagements, but also applies to any unexpected event—the first George Bush, for instance, was heavily criticized for his lack of attention to an earthquake in California, and so was his son for the lack of response to Hurricane Katrina. Barack Obama, on the other hand, was able to take advantage of Hurricane Sandy, and both Ronald Reagan and Bill Clinton underscored their reputations for eloquence as they responded to the explosion of the shuttle *Challenger* and the bombing in Oklahoma City. George W. Bush, whose initial response to the events of September 11, 2001 was widely understood as ineffective, redeemed his leadership when, bullhorn in hand, he assured the nation that "the people who knocked these buildings down will hear all of us soon." Presidents are often at their rhetorical best in response to crisis, and such moments allow for them to authoritatively speak for the united nation.

Crisis presents one kind of ceremonial opportunity. Presidents also have episodic opportunities to make ceremonial addresses. The most frequent of these opportunities are eulogies. Presidential eulogies do the same kind of political work as White House events, but draw a national rather than local audience. Presidents have a wide range of options regarding eulogies. They decide which funerals and memorials they will attend, whether or not they will speak, and so on. And in general, they choose to eulogize those who can be made to stand for the administration, those who represent its understanding of citizenship and national identity. These are not moments to make the case for smaller policy initiatives, but to argue for the broader understanding of politics in which those initiatives are embedded. Presidents eulogize exemplary citizens—so when Abraham Lincoln valorized the dead at Gettysburg for their dedication to the Union, he was also exhorting the living to be so dedicated. Ronald Reagan did much the same kind of thing in remembering the *Challenger* astronauts. And when Barack Obama spoke after the 2011 Tucson shooting, he used the child Christina as a way of envisioning the possibilities of a more civil politics. Presidents can use such occasions to underline the virtues they value, encourage the kind of citizenship that authorizes their own leadership, and symbolically move the nation in the direction they prefer.

In addition to occasional ceremonial and unexpected events, presidents also have episodic opportunities to make overt policy pitches. They can use press conferences, weekly radio addresses, and other signaling events to make policy-based appeals. The beauty of these events, from the president's point of view, is that they have relatively small audiences with relatively narrow concerns. Union members will hear about a president's ideas concerning labor as that news is circulated through newsletters and other kinds of narrowcasting. That same message may go unheard or unattended to by those with other kinds of concerns. Narrowcasting is often seen as a problem for presidential speech because it absorbs considerable presidential time for a small audience. Such speech, however, can be used to the president's advantage.

In episodic communication, then, whether it concerns crisis, ceremony, or policy, the idea is the same: seize the opportunity to make the larger case through example and argument. If these events are treated as trivial or as unconnected to the president's broader agenda, they are wasted opportunities.

Crisis

During times of crisis, no one can command the national stage like the president. When technology fails, as in the case of shuttle disasters, when the nation is attacked or commits troops overseas, as in the cases of Pearl Harbor, 9/11, or the various wars in the Middle East, when there are natural disasters like earthquakes, floods, hurricanes and tornados, whenever the nation is faced with the unexpected and potentially threatening, it looks to the president for interpretation and reassurance. These events are signaled by media coverage and by the necessity for political response. School shootings in Columbine, Colorado, and in Sandy Hook, Connecticut, for example, merited presidential attention. Many other such shootings pass by unremarked by either the president or the media. Presidents respond to crisis either when they decide they should or when the level of media coverage seems to require it.

Crises provide important opportunities for presidents, not least because at such moments they are the focal point of national attention. They can also exploit crisis to ask for—and often receive—more extensive delegations of power. Such was the case, for instance, when FDR assumed broad power in the wake of the Depression and Second World War. Such power, often understood as temporarily ceded to the executive, in reality is rarely, if ever, actually given back. Crisis rhetoric can be used both to reinforce the nation's sense of itself and to advance specific policies.

Presidents both respond to crisis not of their making—caused by terrorists, the weather, and war, for instance—and can create the sense of crisis in order to authorize action—they declare war on poverty or on inflation, for example. Domestic events, such as protests, or even the seemingly simple act of enrolling an African American child in school, can constitute a crisis requiring presidential response. In all of these cases, presidents offer justifications for their leadership and do best when they can place the crisis in the broader context of their overall administrative goals. Crises present opportunities for presidents to unite the nation on their own terms at dramatic moments. There are also other, quieter opportunities for presidents to do the same kind of unifying.

Press Conferences and Interviews

There is an enormous body of work on the presidency and the press. Presidential press conferences are one of the foci of those analyses. Prior to FDR, presidents met with the press rarely, and these meetings tended to be quite formal. Roosevelt changed this as he changed so much else in the executive institution, and he not only increased the frequency of these events but made them informal, even friendly. By the end of the Roosevelt administration, the White House press corps had grown in number and news value. The presidency was a center of political action and the relationship between the president and the media reflected that power. Reagan, whose administration was noted for its ability at "news management," reduced the number of press conferences, and kept the media at a greater distance than had previously been the case. No recent president has seen much utility in expanding their accessibility to the media, and the number of press conferences continues to shrink.

Presidents prefer controlled media—formal speeches, tweets, and other unidirectional forms of communication allow them to can get their message through to the public without the interference or interpretation imposed by the media. They generally limit their communication with the media to the briefings conducted by the press secretary and other administration officials. But a well-conducted press conference can underline a president's rhetorical and policy ability and help mobilize institutional resources for her leadership. John F. Kennedy, for example, excelled at press conferences, and both his wit and intelligence were on display during those occasions. Ronald Reagan took his seriously, and used them to demonstrate his political command over the national government. Despite these examples, presidents are often reluctant to conduct press conferences, seeing them as moments of high risk and little pay off. They are not wrong in this assessment. Press conferences are undoubtedly good for democracy—they are moments when the media are given more or less free rein to hold the president accountable and to put him on the record regarding national policy. It is less clear that presidents see this as an unequivocal benefit.

Signaling Events

As much as presidents dislike the uncontrolled element of press conferences, they still must use the media to reach the American and international public, and often look for more controllable ways of doing this. They can, for example, have limited press encounters, where they give short statement followed by a few questions on a specific topic. Similarly, they can give one-on-one interviews, such as the 2014 encounter between Fox News's Bill O'Reilly and Barack Obama. That interview not only received significant attention before its broadcast but also afterwards, and the judgment from both the Right and the Left seems to have been in Obama's favor. It benefits both the president and the media to present their relationship as adversarial. In reality, that is both posturing—they need one another—and accurate—it's a battle for control over the information the media make available to the public. Presidents are happiest when they exercise the most control over that information. They tend to have the most difficulty when that control is lost.

Presidents can use these opportunities to signal the importance of specific elements of their policy agendas. A president can use the entire administrative apparatus at her disposal to make sure that the media are fed stories that suit the president's agenda. She can release information at times and on terms that she considers favorable. But endeavors to control information are always incomplete and partial. No administration can ever completely control the narratives that circulate about it. And when they fail, those failures are very much on display.

Minimizing Failures

Sometimes, public speech is less about exploiting opportunity and more about minimizing the damage done by family members, staffers, and presidents themselves. This damage ranges from the minor to the impeachable and should be treated accordingly. The least dangerous mistakes are gaffes, those verbal and visual slips to which we are all prone but which, because of the heightened attention the office receives, can be embarrassing to a president. Most gaffes are ephemeral and matter very little. The exceptions matter either because they confirm an existing negative belief about a president or because they apparently contradict a positive belief about her. In a moment that regularly makes the "top ten debate gaffe" lists, for instance, Gerald Ford, intending to underline a strong foreign policy vis-à-vis the Soviet Union, and meaning to note that the United States did not recognize the validity of Soviet domination of Eastern Europe, misspoke, claiming instead that "there is no Soviet dominance of Eastern Europe." On one level, this was trivial. No one could possibly believe that Ford was unaware of the politics of Eastern Europe.

On another level, it was devastating. Ford had never stood for national election and there was considerable uncertainty about his ability to govern. His misstatement here reinforced those fears.

Gaffes can be visual as well as verbal, of course. There are always doubts that Democrats will be militarily weaker than Republicans, for instance, and when Michael Dukakis donned a combat helmet apparently several sizes too large and rode around in a tank during his presidential campaign, he appeared ludicrous rather than competent. And while George W. Bush looked considerably more comfortable in his combat uniform, the visual of his landing on an aircraft carrier with the message "Mission Accomplished" in the background haunted him as the war dragged on. When no high-ranking member of the Obama administration joined the world leaders marching together in solidarity during the aftermath of the Charlie Hebdo killings in 2015, that absence was understood internationally, and acknowledged by Obama, as a mistake.

Presidents strive to maintain a consistent image and gaffes that threaten to reveal the "true" side of a president can work against them. When the famously eloquent and wonkish Barack Obama stumbled over the pronunciation of his new program "MyRA" in his 2014 State of the Union, it created no actual problem for the president. The coverage moved almost immediately to the details of the program. Had the famously inarticulate George W. Bush made the same mistake, it would have been equally unremarkable. In Obama's case, there is too much evidence that he both understands policy and how to talk about it for one glitch to be interesting. In Bush's case, there is too much evidence that he verbally stumbled for it to change public perceptions. And while the racial slurs and strong language revealed in the Watergate tapes undermined Nixon's public image, Bush's aside to his then vice-presidential candidate that a reporter was a "major league asshole" caused nary a ripple, and may have reinforced the belief that he was "a regular guy." A gaffe for one president may go unremarked in another. Gaffes create problems when they contradict what we think we know or when they consistently underline negatives.

But most gaffes are of little importance and can be safely ignored. Actual scandal is much more problematic for presidents. According to recent work by Brandon Rottinghaus, serious damage can be usefully categorized as involving financial malfeasance, political corruption, and personally unethical behavior. In general, he finds, scandals at the national level are relatively short-lived, lasting on average 255 days. Rottinghaus argues that surviving scandal depends on partisan strength in the legislature and the state of the economy. Public approval has no effect, but institutional support matters a great deal. This seems reasonable, given that the public's power to remove officials from office is limited to elections and the power of impeachment resides in Congress. In the case of Bill Clinton's impeachment, for instance, his survival in office had more to do with the number of Democrats in the Senate than his approval among the mass public. Similarly, Ronald Reagan was able to survive the Iran-Contra scandal in part because of Republican strength in Congress. Richard Nixon was unable to survive, on the other hand, because the scope and extent of the illegalities committed by his administration were so great that his legislative support eroded over time. These examples underline the point that the presidential relationship with the public may be an important focus for presidents, but that relationship is determined in part by the institutional structures of government.

This does not mean that presidents have no power over their fate, however. If nothing else is clear about how politicians in general and presidents in particular handle scandal, it is that denial and avoidance do not work, but tend to make matters worse. Once a presidential secret has been uncovered, it is going to be investigated. Presidents would do well to remember the extent of the reporting on the Clinton's involvement in Whitewater and, on the state level, the attention given to the highway closure scandal involving presidential hopeful and New Jersey Governor Chris Christie. Both examples indicate that denials and obfuscations do little to stop reportage. If there is truth to the charges made against a president or presidential candidate, the best response is to confess early and completely. The public is more likely to forgive a mistake than a cover-up, a lesson presidents are singularly poor at learning.

There are numerous options available to presidents in such a circumstance. Kathleen Hall Jamieson and Karlyn Kohrs Campbell note that presidential responses to scandal fall into two categories: the forensic and the personal apologia. Personal apologia are most useful, they note, before formal charges have been made, and, when effective, constitute single, unified responses that shift the blame from the president to the attackers, and present a defense of the president's character. The point here is to defend the presidential ethos as consistent with good leadership. Forsenic defenses, on the other hand, are legalistic responses to formal charges, in which the overarching argument is that even if the president committed the offense in question it does not rise to the level of impeachment.

The label *apologia* can be misleading because they do not always imply apologies. Apologia are speeches of self-defense, broadly understood. They can take at least four forms: denial, bolstering, differentiation, and transcendence. Denial isn't the declaration that the offense was not committed (as when Bill Clinton asserted, "I'm going to say this again. I did not have sexual relations with that woman, Miss Lewinsky"), but is the declaration that there was no intent to commit an offense (as when Ronald Reagan declared, "A few months ago I told the American people I did not trade arms for hostages. My heart and my best intentions still tell me that's true, but the facts and the evidence tell me it is not"). Denial works best when there is a strong relationship between the president and the audience such that arguments relying on the presidential character as defense will prove effective.

Bolstering is the obverse of denial. This defense is predicated on the connection between the president and values important to the audience. When Abraham Lincoln argued he violated the Constitution in order to save the Union, he was associating his actions with the reverence Americans hold for their foundational documents. Similarly, when Richard Nixon attempted to use "national security" as a defense in Watergate, he was (less successfully) employing bolstering. Bolstering will be most effective when the connection between the values and the action being defended are clear.

Differentiation is a form of dissociation, and involves splitting one accusation into two and defending the one that can be understood in the most positive terms. In his famous "Checkers Speech," for instance, vice-presidential candidate Richard Nixon defended himself against accusations that he had been operating an illegal slush fund. Differentiation features among the strategies he used in that speech. He noted, for instance, that "my opposite number for the Vice-Presidency on the Democratic ticket, does have his wife on the pay roll and has had her on his pay roll for the last ten years. Now let me just say this: That is his business, and I am not critical of him for doing that. You will have to pass judgment on that particular point, but I have never done that for this reason: I have found that there are so many deserving stenographers and secretaries in Washington that needed the work I just didn't feel it was right to put my wife on the pay roll." Note how he implicitly accused Lyndon Johnson, his "opposite number," of corruption. Nixon here defined "corruption" in a particular way and then noted that his opponent was guilty of it while he was not. This tactic works best, of course, when the accusations are susceptible to this kind of technical splitting.

Differentiation works by reduction—it makes the accusation smaller and smaller as it is split into parts. Transcendence on the other hand, works by making the issue bigger—it widens the context through which the offense is understood. Thus, the Clinton administration insisted that the president wanted to release documents related to Whitewater, but was prevented from doing so by the requirements of executive privilege. He was not protecting himself, according to this argument, he was sacrificing his own interests in defense of the executive institution.

The example of scandal illustrates the kinds of options available to presidents as they seek to control the national agenda. If they are consistent in their own rhetoric, exploit the opportunities available to them by grounding their specific policies in widely accepted national values, and connecting those policies

and values through clear narratives, they may not earn for themselves reputations for eloquence, but they will be engaging in the
kinds of rhetorical practice that both help them to make sense
out of their own agendas and preferences and communicate them
to members of other governing institutions, the media, and the
mass public.

Conclusion: Presidential Definitions, Presidential Persuasion

The presidency is a peculiar office, not least because it is
imbued with tremendous power and yet presidents find themselves
continually thwarted. The frustrations of this aspect of the office
must be, one imagines, immense. But those frustrations should
never be publicly aired without specific intent. No one is going
to sympathize with the travails of a person continually referred
to as "the most powerful person in the world." Presidents who
fulminate about their frustrations in public are rarely rewarded
for doing so. Those frustrations are inherent in the job. They can
be reduced by understanding the rhetorical aspects of that job,
because that allows presidents to focus on the things public speech
can do and avoid wasting time and energy on the things it cannot.

The lesson of this chapter is decidedly not that presidents
should stop engaging the public through rhetoric. Maintaining a
strong public presence is integral to their leadership. It isn't useful
to think that going on a "swing around the circle" will change
people's beliefs in the short term. But speaking tours and other
events do accomplish some things for a presidential administration. Presidential speech signals the depth of an administration's
commitment to a policy or program to other key governmental
actors. Presidential visits signal the importance of a district, state,
or constituency to the president's governing and electoral coalition, and facilitate the representative function tied to the executive
office. Presidential attention to individual citizens underlines the
ways in which the president understands the nation and the kinds
of citizen she considers integral to it. And presidential speech
legitimates the kinds of authority presidents assume.

Of course, presidents don't have to travel to "go public." They can take advantage of routine rhetorical moments, like inaugurals, State of the Union and other major policy addresses to make their case to Congress, the American public, and international audiences. These are all opportunities for the president to situate her administration in the larger national narrative. The content of these addresses is important. Their style and tone matter as well, for those convey important information about the president and the national government of which she is a part. If the president can convey his ideals and beliefs in narrative form, as for instance, Reagan did with his heavy reliance on the frontier myth, or Bill Clinton did in his tale of being "from a place called Hope," the connection between the policy and the person become clear, more easily understood, and much more easily remembered.

Good presidential persuaders have one thing in common: in general, they took advantage of the opportunities offered by the institution, and they sometimes created new ones. They understood that no event was too small to make the larger case and they connected matters of local concern to issues on the national agenda, spinning rhetorical webs of connectivity. When they place crisis as well as low level policy within the context of their understanding of the nation, they can make the most out of the opportunities available to them.

Suggested Readings

An, Seon-Kyoung and Karla K. Gower. "How do the News Media Frame Crises? A Content Analysis of Crisis News Coverage." *Public Relations Review* 35 (2009): 107–112.

Barilleaux, Ryan J. and Jewerl Maxwell. *Tough Times for the President: Political Adversity and the Sources of Executive Power.* New York: Cambria Press, 2012.

Barrett, Andrew W. "Going Public as a Legislative Weapon: Measuring Presidential Appeals Regarding Specific Legislation." *Presidential Studies Quarterly* 35 (2005): 1–10.

Bennett, W. Lance and David L. Paletz, eds. *Taken by Storm: The Media, Public Opinion, and US Foreign Policy in the Gulf War.* Chicago: University of Chicago Press, 1994.

Benoit, William L. "Image Repair Discourse and Crisis Communication." *Public Relations Review* 23 (1997): 177–186.

Benoit, William L. "Another Visit to the Theory of Image Restoration Strategies." *Communication Quarterly* 48 (2000): 40–43.

Benoit, William L. "President Bush's Image Repair Effort on *Meet the Press*: The Complexities of Defeasibility." *Journal of Applied Communication Research* 34 (2006): 285–306.

Benoit, William L. and Jayne R. Henson. "President Bush's Image Repair Discourse on Hurricane Katrina." *Public Relations Review* 35 (2009): 40–46.

Biesecker, Barbara A. "Rethinking the Rhetorical Situation from within the Thematic of 'Différance,'" *Philosophy & Rhetoric* 22, no. 2 (1989): 110–130.

Bitzer, Lloyd F. "The Rhetorical Situation." *Philosophy & Rhetoric* 25 (1992): 114.

Blumer, Tom. "Geraldo Goes After O'Reilly, Saying he 'Deminimized' Obama in his Week Ago Interview," MRC Newsbusters blog, February 10, 2014, http://newsbusters.org/blogs/tom-blumer/2014/02/10/geraldo-goes-after-oreilly-saying-he-deminimized-obama-his-week-ago-inte

Bostdorff, Denise M. *The Presidency and the Rhetoric of Foreign Crisis.* Columbia: University of South Carolina Press, 1994.

Brace, Paul and Barbara Hinckley. "Presidential Activities from Truman through Reagan: Timing and Impact." *The Journal of Politics* 55(1993): 382–398.

Browne, Stephen H. "'The Circle of Our Felicities': Thomas Jefferson's First Inaugural Address and the Rhetoric of Nationhood." *Rhetoric & Public Affairs* 5 (2002).

Campbell, Karlyn Kohrs and Kathleen Hall Jamieson. *Deeds Done in Words: Presidential Rhetoric and the Genres of Governance.* Chicago, IL: University of Chicago Press, 1990.

Campbell, Karlyn Kohrs and Kathleen Hall Jamieson, eds. *Form and Genre: Shaping Rhetorical Action.* Falls Church, VA: Speech Communication Association, 1978.

Chernus, Ira. *Eisenhower's Atoms for Peace.* College Station: Texas A&M University Press, 2002.

Cherwitz, Richard A. and Kenneth S. Zagacki. "Consummatory versus Justificatory Crisis Rhetoric." *Western Journal of Speech Communication* 50 (1986): 307–324.

Cobb, Michael D. and James H. Kuklinski. "Changing Minds: Political Arguments and Political Persuasion," *American Journal of Political Science* 41, no. 1 (1997): 88–121.

Cohen, Jeffrey E. *Going Local: Presidential Leadership in the Post-Broadcast Age.* New York: Cambridge University Press, 2010.

Cohen, Jeffrey E. "Presidential Rhetoric and the Public Agenda," *American Journal of Political Science* 39 (1995): 87–107.

Condit, Celeste Marie. "Functions of Epideictic: The Boston Massacre Orations as Exemplar." *Communication Quarterly* 33 (1985): 284–299.

Cummins, Jeff. "The President's Domestic Agenda, Divided Government, and the Relationship to the Public Agenda." *American Review of Politics,* 27 (2006): 269–94.

Cummins, Jeff. "State of the Union Addresses and the President's Legislative Success." *Congress & the Presidency,* 37 (2010): 176–199.

Dow, Bonnie J. "The Function of Epideictic and Deliberative Strategies in Presidential Crisis Rhetoric." *Western Journal of Communication* 53 (1989): 294–310.

Edwards, George C. III. *The Strategic President: Persuasion and Opportunity in Presidential Leadership.* Princeton, NJ: Princeton University Press, 2009.

Fisher, Walter R. *Human Communication as Narration: Toward a Philosophy of Reason, Value, and Action.* Columbia: University of South Carolina Press, 1987.

Friedersdorf, Conor. "Bill O'Reilly Just Unwittingly Proved Obama Right," *The Atlantic,* February 7, 2014, http://www.theatlantic.com/politics/archive/2014/02/bill-oreilly-justunwittingly-proved-obama-right/283666/.

Grossman, Michael Baruch and Martha Joynt Kumar. *Portraying the President: The White House and the News Media.* Baltimore: Johns Hopkins University Press, 1981.

Han, Lori Cox. *Governing from Center Stage: White House Communication Strategies during the Television Age of Politics.* Cresskill, NY: Hampton Press, 2001.

Han, Lori Cox. "New Strategies for an Old Medium: The Weekly Radio Addresses of Reagan and Clinton." *Congress & the Presidency: A Journal of Capital Studies,* 33 (2006): 25–45.

Hart, Roderick P., Jay P. Childers, and Colene J. Lind. *Political Tone: How Leaders Talk and Why.* University of Chicago Press, 2013.

Heidt, Stephen. "The Presidency as Pastiche: Atomization, Circulation, and Rhetorical Instability." *Rhetoric & Public Affairs* 15 (2012): 623–633.

Iyengar, Shanto and Adam Simon. "News Coverage of the Gulf Crisis and Public Opinion: A Study of Agenda-Setting, Priming, and Framing." *Communication Research* 20 (1993): 365–383.

Jacobs, Lawrence R. "Communicating from the White House: Presidential Narrowcasting and the National Interest." *The Executive Branch,* edited by Joel D. Auberbach and Mark A. Peterson (Oxford: Oxford University Press, 2005): 174–208.

Jamieson, Kathleen Hall. *Eloquence in an Electronic Age: The Transformation of Political Speechmaking.* New York: Oxford University
Press, 1988.

Jones, John M. and Robert C. Rowland. "The Weekly Radio Addresses
of President Ronald Reagan." *Journal of Radio Studies* 7 (2000):
257–281.

Kernell, Samuel. *Going Public: New Strategies of Presidential Leadership.* 4th ed.. Washington, DC: CQ Press, 2006.

Kiewe, Amos. *The Modern Presidency and Crisis Rhetoric.* New York:
Praeger Publishers, 1994.

Kumar, Martha Joynt. *Managing the President's Message: The White
House Communications Operation.* Baltimore: Johns Hopkins
University Press, 2010.

Kurr, Jeff. "The Construction of Digital Borders in Obama's Enhanced
State of the Union." paper presented at the annual meeting of the
Rhetoric Society of America, 2014.

Kuypers, Jim A. *Presidential Crisis Rhetoric and the Press in the Post-
Cold War World.* New York: Greenwood Publishing Group, 1997.

Lang, Gladys Engel and Kurt Lang. "Polling on Watergate: The Battle
for Public Opinion." *Public Opinion Quarterly* 44 (1980): 530–547.

Lewis, William F. "Telling America's Story: Narrative Form and
the Reagan Presidency." *Quarterly Journal of Speech* 73 (1987):
280–302.

Lim, Elvin T. *The Anti-intellectual Presidency: The Decline of Presidential Rhetoric from George Washington to George W. Bush.* New
York: Oxford University Press, 2008.

Lim, Elvin T. "The Presidency and the Media: Two Faces of Democracy." In *The Presidency and the Political System,* edited by Michael
Nelson. 10th ed. Washington, DC: CQ Press, 2013. 258–271.

Lucas, Stephen E. "Genre Criticism and Historical Context: The Case
of George Washington's First Inaugural Address," *Quarterly Journal
of Speech* 41, no. 1 (1986): 354–370.

Lucas, Stephen E. and Martin J. Medhurst,"Top 100 Speeches of
the Twentieth Century." http://americanrhetoric.com/newtop-
100speeches.htm

Medhurst, Martin J. *Dwight D. Eisenhower: Strategic Communicator.*
Westport, CT: Greenwood Press, 1993.

Medhurst, Martin J. "Reconceptualizing Rhetorical History: Eisenhower's Farewell Address." *Quarterly Journal of Speech* 80 (1994):
195–218.

Medhurst, Martin J. "Atoms for Peace and Nuclear Hegemony: The
Rhetorical Structure of a Cold War Campaign." *Armed Forces &
Society* 23 (1997): 571–59.

Medhurst, Martin J. "Eisenhower and the Crusade for Freedom: The Rhetorical Origins of a Cold War Campaign." *Presidential Studies Quarterly* 27 (1997): 646–661.

Medhurst, Martin J., Robert L. Ivie, Philip Wander, and Robert L. Scott. *Cold War Rhetoric: Strategy, Metaphor, and Ideology*. East Lansing: Michigan State University Press, 2012.

Murphy, John M. "Our Mission and Our Moment': George W. Bush and September 11." *Rhetoric and Public Affairs* 6 (2003): 607–632.

Noonan, Peggy. *What I saw at the Revolution: A Political Life in the Reagan Era*. New York: Random House, 2003.

Parry-Giles, Shawn J. and Trevor ParryGiles. "Collective Memory, Political Nostalgia, and the Rhetorical Presidency: Bill Clinton's Commemoration of the March on Washington, August 28, 1998." *Quarterly Journal of Speech* 86 (2000): 417–437.

Paulson, Jon. "Theodore Roosevelt and the Rhetoric of Citizenship: On Tour in New England, 1902." *Communication Quarterly* 50 (2002): 123–134.

Ritter, Kurt. and Martin J. Medhurst, eds. *Presidential Speechwriting: From the New Deal to the Reagan Revolution and Beyond*. College Station: Texas A&M University Press, 2004.

Rottinghaus, Brandon. "Surviving Scandal: The Institutional and Political Dynamics of National and State Executive Scandals." *PS: Political Science and Politics* 47 (2014): 131–140.

Sigelman, Lee. "Presidential Inaugurals: The Modernization of a Genre." *Political Communication* 13 (1996).

Simon, Dennis M. and Charles W. Ostrom, "The Impact of Televised Speeches and Foreign Travel on Presidential Approval." *Public Opinion Quarterly* 53 (1989): 58–82.

Smith, Craig R. *Confessions of a Presidential Speechwriter*. East Lansing: Michigan State University Press, 2014.

Stuckey, Mary E. *Slipping the Surly Bonds: Reagan's Challenger Address*. College Station: Texas A&M University Press, 2006.

Tenpas, Katherine Dunn. "The State of the Union Address." In *The President's Words: Speeches and Speechmaking in the Modern White House* edited by M. Nelson and R. L. Riley, 147–205. Lawrence: University Press of Kansas, 2010.

Teten, Ryan L. "Evolution of the Modern Rhetorical Presidency: Presidential Presentation and Development of the State of the Union Address." *Presidential Studies Quarterly* 33 (2003): 333–346.

Vatz, Richard E. "The Myth of the Rhetorical Situation." *Philosophy and Rhetoric* 6 (1973): 154–161.

Ware, B. Lee and Wil A. Linkugel. "They Spoke in Defense of Themselves: On the Generic Criticism of Apologia." *Quarterly Journal of Speech* 59 (1973): 273–283.

White, Graham J. *FDR and the Press*. Chicago: University of Chicago Press, 1979.

Winfield, Betty Houchin. *FDR and the News Media*. Columbia University Press, 1994.

Zarefsky, David. "Lyndon Johnson Redefines 'Equal Opportunity': The Beginnings of Affirmative Action." *Communication Studies* 31 (1980): 85–94.

CONCLUSION
PRESIDENTS AND THEIR RHETORIC

At least in part, presidents seek the office because of the things it allows them to accomplish. They have policy goals and want the opportunity to enact those goals as legislation. But they also want to be president because the institution involves more than just policy. The presidency is a nexus of symbolic meaning and social as well as political power, and every president is afforded the opportunity to modulate the contours of what it means to be president and what it means to be American. Rhetoric is the vehicle through which that modulation occurs. We think of rhetoric as operating at those moments when the president eloquently occupies the grandest stages of our national politics, offering inspiration, hope, and reassurance. But presidential rhetoric also works in the nooks and crannies of the office, often when the audience is smaller and the opposition less vocal.

The way we think of rhetoric tells us a great deal about how we think of national politics. The idea that rhetoric ought to work as a one-way method of persuasion implies a certain top-down view of politics in which elites form messages designed to convince followers to accept their leadership. A more democratically-oriented view of rhetoric offers both speakers and their audience agency over the design, reception, interpretation, and ultimate social consequences of public speech. Analysts who mistrust the electorate are also likely to mistrust rhetoric, considering it a nefarious way of misleading the ignorant and ill-informed. On the other hand, if one assumes that voters exercise some agency over the communication that governs political relationships, then it follows that the voters have some ability to understand, if not influence, the terms of those relationships.

When presidents offer consistent narratives of the nation and of their role within it, no occasion is too small to make the larger case. Presidential rhetoric is thus best understood as cumulative—as a means of constituting the nation, the institution, and the administration over time. Such an understanding is hard to measure by public opinion polls or through the success or failure of specific policy proposals. It is more useful to think of rhetoric in this sense as involving more or less equal parts policy advocacy, the creation and maintenance of institutional capacities for governance, the provision of inventional resources, national representation, and civic engagement. While the environment in which these rhetorical actions take place has changed over time, the logic governing presidential rhetoric remains fundamentally the same. In this final chapter, I first discuss my previous arguments about the various capacities of presidential rhetoric and then conclude with some ideas about how "good" rhetoric might therefore be understood.

Rhetorical Capacities

The presidency is an office with many resources, both material and symbolic. Presidents are often better at understanding and mobilizing the material resources at their disposal and may overlook the ways in which their symbolic resources may be used to advance their political and policy goals.

Policy Advocacy

As I have reiterated throughout this volume, there is very good evidence that presidents who "go public" in order to mobilize the mass public to force policy change, presidents who think that they can do a "swing around the circle" to forge short-term opinion change on narrowly defined issues, are unlikely to succeed. This does not mean that presidents can never influence public opinion, but that such influence is unlikely in the short term or on a specific issue. Presidents can, however, influence public opinion in a broader sense. They can shape the ways in which we conceive of the nation and the role of government within it. Bill Clinton's 1996 declaration that "the era of big government is over," for example, probably did little to change people's minds about "big government," but it did signal an important change in how that government would be understood as influencing American policy-making.

Presidents are expected to make the public case for their policy proposals, and indeed it is possible to understand democratic government in just such terms: in democracies, we require our leaders to make public arguments in public forums for public action. The increased public presence of the president therefore signals a certain democratization of the political world. Citizens as audiences became more important to the decision-making processes of government as the presidency assumed a more central representative role. There is no question but that presidents sought to include citizens less because they were unceasingly dedicated to democratizing national government and more because they were seeking leverage over the policy process and specifically were attempting to dominate Congress. This has worked more at the margins than in the main. But the fact remains that the mass public is now an important element in policymaking.

This increased dependence on the mass public as a source of political legitimacy is complicated by the increasing diversity and fractiousness of that mass public. When Roosevelt spoke to his nation, his audience was limited. His politics were, for his day, reasonably inclusive. They left out large numbers of Americans—most starkly, he left Jim Crow entirely untouched. Later presidents, both those who favored the expansion of the polity and those who preferred it to be more restricted, encountered a nation that increasingly understood itself in terms of its diversity, organized itself on those terms, and began making claims upon government. Appeals that once would have passed without comment became matters of serious dispute and presidents who wanted to wield power, and who sometimes relied on these organized citizens to help them do so, also had to contend with the pressure that came along with that use.

Presidents must therefore advocate their policies in public, and they must do so knowing that this advocacy will mobilize opponents as well as supporters and that sometimes it can be hard to tell the difference between members of those two groups. Their public speech is, of course, an important element of this advocacy, but it cannot guarantee success, and it is better understood as contributing to a president's political success in less obviously direct ways.

Institutional Capacity

Contemporary presidents are, by their institutional nature, power-seekers. But in a nation that values its commitment to republican government, it is hard to make unabashed claims to power. Assumptions of power must always be argued for, legitimated, and authorized, all of which are deeply rhetorical processes. By offering definitions of national policy based on the mobilization of foundational national values, presidents not only explain and justify their political preferences, but also their own exercise of power. Andrew Jackson defended his war on the National Bank as necessary for the protection of democracy. It was not incidental that in making this claim, he implicitly argued that the president, not Congress, was the best defender of the nation and should be empowered to act in the nation's behalf. Presidents in this century make similar claims all of time. Lyndon Johnson argued in the aftermath of the violence in Selma, Alabama, "There is no Negro problem. There is no Southern problem. There is no Northern problem. There is only an American problem. And we are met here tonight as Americans—not as Democrats or Republicans—we are met here as Americans to solve that problem." In defining the problem this way, he was also arguing that national problems required national action—and national action meant presidential leadership.

Rhetoric aimed at individual policy areas, then, is also aimed at increasing institutional capacities for addressing political issues. Even presidents like Ronald Reagan, who vowed to "get government off the backs of the American people," also argued for presidential authority vis-à-vis that of Congress, for only if the president had power could he curb the actions of his theoretically co-equal branch. Presidents, regardless of ideology or partisan affiliation, want to maintain or increase the powers of the office. They cannot do that without rhetorically justifying the assumption and use of their political and administrative power.

Inventional Resources

No matter how much power presidents manage to accrue, it is never enough to accomplish their goals or those of their supporters. And presidents are constantly aware of the pressure of time—they have four, at most eight years to turn their promises into policy. Given the exigencies of the legislative process, this presents any number of challenges to presidential ambitions. Presidents should, of course, try to accomplish as much of their agenda as possible. Some administrations are more easily able to do this than others, both because of individual and contextual factors. Those who face immediate difficulties, however, might benefit from thinking of themselves in the context of institutional and political history. Politics is always contingent, and few arguments are ever finally settled. Every policy, every piece of legislation, is one move in the longer arc of national political argument.

When viewed this way, presidential rhetoric both calls upon the legacies of previous presidents and provides resources for those who come later. One sign of the prevailing dissension in the Republican Party, for example, is the venom with which they dispute the "real" meaning of Ronald Reagan's legacy. National history is malleable and subject to a variety of interpretations. Nearly all presidents cite Thomas Jefferson to authorize some element of their agenda, for example, and they are all likely to avail themselves of myths related to the frontier and national progress. Presidents who understand themselves as part of an ongoing conversation about the direction of that progress will actually find themselves both having access to and leaving behind them a richer repertoire of narratives.

Representation

Presidents do not just speak to us, they also speak for us. When they honor members of the public, when the invite citizens to the White House, when they visit small towns and big cities and all the places in between, they are doing more than simply asking for our vote, our support, our influence over members of Congress. They are reminding us of the length and breadth and complexity of the nation they govern, and they are underlining the expanses of inclusion and also its limits. When Franklin Roosevelt appointed Frances Perkins to his cabinet, it was more than just a recognition that women had been instrumental in his election. When Ronald Reagan lifted a glass with blue collar workers in a local pub, he was not accurately portraying some of his economic policies, but he was appealing—and doing so successfully—to people who became known as Reagan Democrats. When Bill Clinton agreed that "Don't Ask, Don't Tell" would govern the role of LGBTQ people in the military, he was also making a powerful statement about their role in the broader American polity. When Barack Obama, after a long period of internal debate, decided to support same-sex marriage, he was expanding that role. Presidents "go local" as part of their efforts to influence governmental action, and there is some evidence that it does in fact do so. In doing so, however, they are also serving as important representatives of the nation, reminding the citizens that they too have a role in public life, even if that role is largely symbolic.

Civic Engagement

Pundits and citizens alike talk as if we want presidents to encourage more civic dialogue, inform us on the issues of the day, create national conversations, foster dissent, and forge out of those processes a national consensus. But this hope runs counter to political reality. We do not judge presidents on the quality of the national conversations that occurred while they were in office, but on the extent to which they were able to enact policy. That ability is not a consequence of the amount of debate their activities encouraged. In fact, getting legislation passed may depend on managing to minimize or avoid debate entirely.

Presidents, in general, want to dominate the communicative flow between government and the people. They favor controllable forms of media like speeches and media events over less controllable ones like press conferences and debates. It works to their advantage when they have a consistent narrative that explains their policies in terms of national values and myths. If we understand the president's task as primarily that of educating the public, much of their rhetoric falls into that category. But if we want presidents to engage the public, that task assumes more equality between the president and the public than they are likely to concede—and if they do concede to a more equal relationship in the name of democratizing the office, they are likely to be criticized for failing to lead. The relationship between the presidency and civic engagement is fraught with contradictions, reflecting the ways in which eighteenth century documents continue to inflect contemporary modes of governance.

Creating "Good" Rhetoric

If we understand rhetoric as more than enabling short-term changes in public opinion directed at specific policies, then presidential rhetoric becomes understood as an integral part of governing rather than as an occasional tool of it. In what follows, I offer the lessons that follow directly from the preceding discussions.

First, the executive institution offers both rhetorical opportunities and resources. The genres of presidential discourse not only map the history of the office, but also provide examples of how to meet the public and institutional expectations it requires. All presidents will give at least one inaugural speech, address Congress yearly at the State of the Union and occasionally on other topics, and offer vetoes, pardons, and other forms of standardized speech. All presidents will encounter crisis. Good presidential orators will, at a minimum, largely conform to the expectations of these genres, but will not do so in formulaic ways. Because the office is both institutional and individual, every president will bring her own personality, history, and unique set of narratives to the White House. They were elected, in part, because the narratives based on those individual attributes proved more compelling than that of the opposition. Crafting a narrative that responds to the specific occasion while underlining the specific themes of the administration ought always to be the rhetorical goal.

There ought, for instance, to be good reasons behind a policy choice. That choice should also be consistent with the president's agenda and public character. It should be conveyed in the president's own idiom. When given the chance to speak about policy, the accompanying narrative ought to be appropriate to the policy and infused with a sense of which national values are embodied in that policy. These values are malleable. Republicans Dwight Eisenhower, Ronald Reagan, and George W. Bush all talked about "freedom," and meant different things by that word, which they used to authorize different policy choices. But they were all convincing, if their policy success is any indication, in their own contexts. Part of that success is attributable to the ways in which they contextualized their preferences.

So the second lesson is that no occasion is too small to make the larger argument. Presidents meeting with Boy Scouts can make of them an example of the extracurricular activities they wish to defend as part of their education program, or can avail themselves of a meeting with factory workers to make implicit arguments about the changing nature of the American work force. In many ways, the most effective presidential administrations will be those that are the most focused. However, focus does not, necessarily imply that there will be a limited agenda—surely few presidents were as capacious in their agendas, for example, as Franklin D. Roosevelt or Bill Clinton. But both these presidents, like the more narrowly interested Ronald Reagan, understood that they needed to present their policies as pieces of a larger whole, and they rarely lost sight of that whole. Rhetorically effective presidents, then, bring the same rhetorical energy to the small moments, with the limited audiences, as to the larger occasions. In those small moments, the personal consequences of the bigger policy picture can sometimes be seen more clearly. Treating those moments as trivial is to miss important opportunities to convey the sense and meaning of administrative practices and preferences.

Effective presidential communicators therefore strive not to miss opportunities, but they also recognize the limits of those opportunities—control over language, meaning, and "the national narrative" are necessarily always incomplete. By keeping their press secretary informed, by organizing their communication office and the rest of their administration such that staffers are aware of and in agreement with the president's vision, the chances that the narrative will be consistent are improved. Internal dissension and strife virtually guarantee that the public perception will include indications of a "divided White House." Presidents have significant power but they cannot command either the loyalty of their own staff or of the media. When they do not get the coverage they think they deserve, the absolute worst thing they can do is to make the resulting frustration public or to seek to stop staffers from making their issues public. Such efforts become the story, further driving the narrative away from the story preferred by the White House. George H. W. Bush's famous contempt for "the vision thing," became a story, highlighting not the president's dedication to policy, but his failure as a communicator. Jimmy Carter suffered from a similar problem. Whenever possible, presidents should strive to avoid the distractions caused by their incomplete control of the political world and focus on the larger story their administration is seeking to tell.

Presidents therefore need to recognize that their rhetoric is collective. The president's words get more attention than anyone else's in the administration, but those words will have more staying power if the administration speaks with a unified voice. The vice-president, cabinet members, staffers, family members, and others associated with the administration can hurt the president by offering opinions that differ from those espoused by the president. They can also help by underlining key points, phrases, and definitions. The presidency is a collective institution. Its rhetoric should also be collective.

This means that presidents and their staffs need to be patient. It is easy to assume that they can change the political context by giving a speech or even a series of speeches, that a well-planned media campaign can change the minds of the voting public. This is not only easy, it is also generally wrong. Even Franklin Roosevelt, a masterly communicator if there ever was one, had limited success with such tactics. Consider, for instance, the fact that the "Great Debate" over the role the US should play in the developing European war raged from at least 1935 until the bombing of Pearl Harbor in December, 1941. The president took a more or less active role in that debate for years before the passage of Lend-Lease definitively declared American intentions, and Axis actions had as much to do with the changes in public opinion as anything else. But Roosevelt defined the meaning of those actions and thus also the meaning of the war. He did so through years of patient argument, stating and restating his case, until his terms became the terms through which the conflict was understood. Those definitions are with us still.

Not all presidential definitions will have such staying power. But all presidents have the same opportunity to define the terms through which policy debates will be understood. Partisan battles, battles between Congress and the Executive (which, given divided government are sometimes the same thing as partisan battles) are often battles fought over the definitions of issues. We argue over whether wars are fought in the name of democracy or are merely "blood for oil"; we wonder if same sex marriage is a civil right or an abrogation of rights; we challenge the idea that abortion is "prolife" with the argument that it is integral to a woman's "right to choose." Politics involves matters that are always contingent, always subject to interpretation, always liable to linguistic frames. Presidents who want their frames to influence, even dominate the national discourse cannot assume that this process happens easily, quickly, or without a great deal of support from other national voices. Public argument in a democracy is a cacophony. Presidents must speak loudly, often, and on the same themes if they are to be heard above it.

This means that technology matters. Presidents may get less national attention than they once did, although the argument for a diminished presidential presence is, I think, overstated. While we once had fewer media competing for our attention, that does not necessarily mean national attention was therefore necessarily concentrated. When Roosevelt was the only voice on the radio, or when Kennedy was the only image on the television, if citizens were tuned in to either, they heard and saw the president. But they may not have tuned in. Even if their radio or TV was on, citizens may not have been fully attentive to them. Even in a more limited media environment, their children cried, their dinners needed cooking, their neighbors may have stopped by. Life for most citizens has always been full of distractions, and getting the nation's sustained attention focused on policy details has challenged every president, no matter how their arguments were transmitted. Presidents do not have to master any one medium. They do have to maintain a presence in all of them. So it is unsurprising that email inboxes are full of messages from Obama's campaign team, "Obama for America," long after the election was decided. It does not surprise that Obama, his wife, and even his dog tweet. Obama, like Roosevelt, Kennedy, and Reagan, understands the value of a public presence.

And Obama, like other presidents who take their communication seriously, uses that presence to convey more than policy proposals, but to establish and maintain his public image, or ethos. Rhetorically adept presidents are not content to try and recreate history. They do not seek to sound like earlier presidents, however much they may admire and evoke them. They speak in their own voice and in so doing they not only speak to us as a nation but also for us as a nation. Presidents are not all-powerful, and there are many things they cannot do. But their conduct in office is so contestable precisely because they represent us to ourselves and to the world. They tell us who we are and who we might hope to become. Politics involves the institutions and processes of our national life. It is conducted through talk and performed through the rhetoric of our presidents.

Suggested Readings

Beasley, Vanessa B., Robert B. Asen, Diane M. Blair, Stephen J. Hartnett, Karla K. Leeper, and Jennifer R. Mercieca, "Report of the National Task Force on the Presidency and Deliberative Democracy," pp. 251–271, in eds., Martin J. Medhurst and James Arnt Aune. *The Prospect of Presidential Rhetoric*. College Station: Texas A&M University Press, 2008.

Campbell, Karlyn Kohrs, and Kathleen Hall Jamieson, eds. *Form and Genre: Shaping Rhetorical Action*. Falls Church, VA: Speech Communication Association, 1978.

Campbell, Karlyn Kohrs, and Kathleen Hall Jamieson. *Presidents Creating the Presidency: Deeds Done in Words*. Chicago: University of Chicago Press, 2008.

Cohen, Jeffrey E. *Going Local: Presidential Leadership in the Post-Broadcast Age*. Cambridge University Press, 2010.

Driver, Peter. "Reagan's Real Legacy," *The Nation*, February 4, 2011, http://www.thenation.com/article/158321/reagans-real-legacy#

Edwards, George C. III. *At the Margins: Presidential Leadership of Congress*. New Haven, CT: Yale University Press, 1989.

Edwards, George C. III *On Deaf Ears*. New Haven, CT: Yale University Press, 2003.

Edwards, George C. III *The Strategic President: Persuasion and Opportunity in Presidential Leadership*. Princeton, NJ: Princeton University Press, 2009.

Finnegan, Cara. "Picturing the President: Obama and the Visual Politics of White House Art," *The Rhetoric of Heroic Expectations: Establishing the Obama Presidency* ed. Justin Vaughan and Jennifer Mercieca. College Station: Texas A&M University Press, 2014.

Kernell, Samuel. *Going Public: New Strategies of Presidential Leadership* fourth edition. Washington, DC: CQ Press, 2006 [1986].

Skowronek, Stephen. *The Politics Presidents Make: Leadership from John Adams to Bill Clinton*. Harvard University Press, 1993.

Stuckey, Mary E. "The 'Great Debate': The Battle over American Neutrality, 1936–1941," ed. Martin J. Medhurst, *A Rhetorical History of the United States, Volume 8: World War II and the Cold War*. East Lansing, Michigan State University Press, forthcoming.

BIBLIOGRAPHY

Allen, Mark. *Why Romney Lost the 2012 Election.* Amazon: Kindle, 2012.

Anderson, Karrin Vasby, and Kristy Horn Sheeler. *Woman President: Confronting Postfeminist Political Culture.* College Station: Texas A&M University Press, 2013.

Anthony, Carl Sferrazza. *First Ladies: The Saga of the Presidents' Wives and Their Power.* New York: Morrow, 1991.

Arnold, Peri. *Making the Managerial Presidency: Comprehensive Reorganization Planning, 1905–1996.* Lawrence: University Press of Kansas, 1998.

Azari, Julia, R. *Delivering the People's Message: The Changing Politics of the Presidential Mandate.* Ithaca: Cornell University Press, 2014.

Balz, Dan. *Obama vs, Romney: 'The Take' on Election 2012.* Washington, DC: *The Washington Post,* 2013.

Barber, James David. *The Presidential Character: Predicting Performance in the White House.* 2nd ed. Englewood Cliffs, NJ: Prentice Hall, 1977.

Beasley, Vanessa. *You, the People: American National Identity in Presidential Rhetoric.* College Station: Texas A&M University Press, 2004.

Beasley, Vanessa B., Robert B. Asen, Diane M. Blair, Stephen J. Hartnett, Karla K. Leeper, and Jennifer R. Mercieca. "Report of the National Task Force on the Presidency and Deliberative Democracy." In *The Prospect of Presidential Rhetoric,* edited by Martin J. Medhurst and James Arnt Aune, 251–71. College Station: Texas A&M University Press, 2008.

Becker, Lee B., and Tudor Vlad. "News Organizations and Routines." *The Handbook of Journalism Studies,* edited by Karrin Wahl-Jorgensen and Thomas Hanitzsch (Routledge, 2009): 59–72.

Bennett, Lance W. "The Burglar Alarm That Just Keeps Ringing: A Response to Zaller." *Political Communication* 20 (2003): 131–38.

Benson, Thomas W. *Writing JFK: Presidential Rhetoric and the Press in the Bay of Pigs Crisis.* College Station: Texas A&M University Press, 2004.

Berry, Jeffrey M., and Clyde Wilcox. *The Interest Group Society.* 5th ed. New York: Pearson, 2008.

Biesecker, Barbara A. "Rethinking the Rhetorical Situation from within the Thematic of 'Différance,'"*Philosophy & Rhetoric* 22, no. 2 (1989): 110–130.

Bitzer, Lloyd F. "The Rhetorical Situation." *Philosophy & Rhetoric* 25 (1992): 1–14.

Blumer, Tom. "Geraldo Goes after O'Reilly, Saying He 'Deminimized' Obama in his Week Ago Interview." MRC Newsbusters blog. February 10, 2014. http://newsbusters.org/blogs/tom-blumer/2014/02/10/geraldo-goes-after-oreilly-saying-he-deminimized-obama-his-week-ago-inte

Bostdorff, Denise M. *The Presidency and the Rhetoric of Foreign Crisis.* Columbia: University of South Carolina Press, 1994.

Brace, Paul, and Barbara Hinckley. "Presidential Activities from Truman through Reagan: Timing and Impact." *The Journal of Politics* 55 (1993): 382–98.

Browne, Stephen H. "'The Circle of Our Felicities': Thomas Jefferson's First Inaugural Address and the Rhetoric of Nationhood." *Rhetoric & Public Affairs* 5 (2002): 409–38.

Bucy, Erik P., and Maria Elizabeth Grabe. "Taking Television Seriously: A Sound and Image Bite Analysis of Presidential Campaign Coverage, 1992–2004." *Journal of Communication* 57 (2007): 652–75.

Burke, Kenneth. *A Rhetoric of Motives.* Berkeley: University of California Press, 1969.

Burns, Lisa M. *First Ladies and the Fourth Estate: Press Framing of Presidential Wives.* DeKalb: Northern Illinois University Press, 2008.

Campbell, Karlyn Kohrs, and Kathleen Hall Jamieson, eds. *Form and Genre: Shaping Rhetorical Action.* Falls Church, VA: Speech Communication Association, 1978.

Campbell, Karlyn Kohrs, and Kathleen Hall Jamieson. "Inaugurating the Presidency." *Presidential Studies Quarterly* 15, no. 2 (1985): 394–411.

Campbell, Karlyn Kohrs, and Kathleen Hall Jamieson. *Presidents Creating the Presidency: Deeds Done in Words.* Chicago: University of Chicago Press, 2008.

Caroli, Betty Boyd. *First Ladies.* New York: Oxford University Press, 2003.

Ceaser, James W., Glen E. Thurow, Jeffrey K. Tulis, and Joseph M. Besette, "The Rise of the Rhetorical Presidency." *Presidential Studies Quarterly* 11 (1981): 158–71.

Chernus, Ira. *Eisenhower's Atoms for Peace.* College Station: Texas A&M University Press, 2002.

Cherwitz, Richard A., and Kenneth S. Zagacki. "Consummatory versus Justificatory Crisis Rhetoric." *Western Journal of Speech Communication* 50 (1986): 307–24.

Cobb, Michael D., and James H. Kuklinski. "Changing Minds: Political Arguments and Political Persuasion." *American Journal of Political Science* 41, no. 1 (1997): 88–121.

Cohen, Jeffrey E. *Going Local: Presidential Leadership in the Post-Broadcast Age.* Cambridge: Cambridge University Press, 2009.

Cohen, Jeffrey E. "Presidential Rhetoric and the Public Agenda." *American Journal of Political Science* 39 (1995): 87–107.

Condit, Celeste Marie. "Functions of Epideictic: The Boston Massacre Orations as Exemplar." *Communication Quarterly* 33 (1985): 284–99.

Cummins, Jeff. "The President's Domestic Agenda, Divided Government, and the Relationship to the Public Agenda." *American Review of Politics* 27 (2006): 269–94.

Cummins, Jeff. "State of the Union Addresses and the President's Legislative Success." *Congress & the Presidency* 37 (2010): 176–99.

Dalleck, Robert. *Ronald Reagan: The Politics of Symbolism.* Cambridge, MA: Harvard University Press, 1987.

Davis, Vincent, ed. *The Post-Imperial Presidency.* Piscataway, NJ: Transaction, 1980.

Denton, Robert E. *The Primetime Presidency of Ronald Reagan: The Era of the Television Presidency.* New York: Praeger, 1988.

Donaldson, Sam. *Hold On, Mr. President!* New York: Random House, 1987.

Dow, Bonnie J. "The Function of Epideictic and Deliberative Strategies in Presidential Crisis Rhetoric." *Western Journal of Communication* 53 (1989): 294–310.

Drury, Jeffrey P. Mehltretter. *Speaking with the People's Voice: How Presidents Invoke Public Opinion.* College Station: Texas A&M University Press, 2014.

Edwards, George C. III. *At the Margins: Presidential Leadership of Congress.* New Haven: Yale University Press, 1989.

Edwards, George C. III. *On Deaf Ears.* New Haven: Yale University Press, 2003.

Edwards, George C. III. *The Strategic President: Persuasion and Opportunity in Presidential Leadership.* Princeton: Princeton University Press, 2009.

Edwards, George C. III, and B. Dan Wood. "Who Influences Whom? The President, Congress, and the Media." *American Political Science Review* 93 (1999): 237–344.

Edwards, Jason A. *Navigating the Post-Cold War World: President Clinton's Foreign Policy Rhetoric.* Lanham, MD: Rowman & Littlefield, 2008.

Eisinger, Robert M. *The Evolution of Presidential Polling.* New York: Cambridge University Press, 2003.

Engels, Jeremy. *Enemyship: Democracy and Counter-Revolution in the Early Republic.* East Lansing: Michigan State University Press, 2010.

Entman, Robert M. "Cascading Activation: Contesting the White House's Frame after 9/11." *Political Communication* 20 (2003): 413–32.

Entman, Robert M. "Framing: Toward Clarification of a Fractured Paradigm." *Journal of Communication* 43 (1993): 51–58.

Esbaugh-Soha, Matthew. *The President's Speeches: Beyond "Going Public."* Boulder, CO: Lynne Reiner Publishers, 2006.

Evans, Rowland, and Robert Novak. *Lyndon B. Johnson: The Exercise of Power.* New York: New American Library, 1966.

Fahnestock, Jeanne. *Rhetorical Style: The Uses of Language in Persuasion.* New York: Oxford, 2011.

Fenno, Richard F. *Home Style: House Members in their Districts.* Boston: Little, Brown, 1978.

Finnegan, Cara. "Picturing the President: Obama and the Visual Politics of White House Art." In *The Rhetoric of Heroic Expectations: Establishing the Obama Presidency,* edited by Justin Vaughan and Jennifer Mercieca, 209–34 College Station: Texas A&M University Press, 2014.

Fisher, Louis. *President and Congress: Power and Policy.* New York: Free Press, 1972.

Fisher, Walter R. *Human Communication as Narration: Toward a Philosophy of Reason, Value, and Action.* Columbia: University of South Carolina Press, 1987.

Fisher, Walter R. "Rhetorical Fiction and the Presidency." *Quarterly Journal of Speech* 66 (1980): 119–26.

Friedersdorf, Conor. "Bill O'Reilly Just Unwittingly Proved Obama Right." February 7, 2014. http://www.theatlantic.com/politics/archive/2014/02/bill-oreilly-just-unwittingly-proved-obama-right/283666/.

Gilberg, Sheldon, Chaim Eyal, Maxwell McCombs, and David Nichols. "The State of the Union and the Press Agenda." *Journalism Quarterly* 57 (1980): 584–88.

Glavin, Daniel J. *Presidential Party Building: Dwight D. Eisenhower to George W. Bush.* Princeton: Princeton University Press, 2009.

Goodale, Greg. "The Presidential Sound: From Orotund to Instructional Speech, 1892–1912." *Quarterly Journal of Speech* 96 (2010): 164–84.

Gross, David. *The Secret History of Emotion: From Aristotle's Rhetoric to Modern Brain Science.* Chicago: University of Chicago Press, 2007.

Grossman, Michael Baruch, and Martha Joynt Kumar. *Portraying the President: The White House and the News Media.* Baltimore: Johns Hopkins University Press, 1981.

Grover, William F. *The President as Prisoner: A Structural Critique of the Carter and Reagan Years.* Albany: SUNY Press, 1989.

Hager, Gregory L., and Terry Sullivan. "President-Centered and Presidency-Centered Explanations of Presidential Public Activity." *American Journal of Political Science* 38, no. 4 (1994): 1079–1103.

Han, Lori Cox. *Governing from Center Stage: White House Communication Strategies during the Television Age of Politics.* Cresskill, NY: Hampton Press, 2001.

Han, Lori Cox. "New Strategies for an Old Medium: The Weekly Radio Addresses of Reagan and Clinton." *Congress & the Presidency: A Journal of Capital Studies* 33 (2006): 25–45.

Han, Lori Cox, and Diane J. Heith. *In the Public Domain: Presidents and the Challenges of Public Leadership.* New York: SUNY Press, 2005.

Hart, Roderick P. *Seducing America: How Television Charms the Modern Voter.* Thousand Oaks, CA: Sage, 1998.

Hart, Roderick P. *The Sound of Leadership: Presidential Communication in the Modern Age.* Chicago: University of Chicago Press, 1989.

Hart, Roderick P., Jay P. Childers, and Colene J. Lind. *Political Tone: How Leaders Talk and Why.* Chicago: University of Chicago Press, 2013.

Hartnett, Stephen John. *Democratic Dissent and the Cultural Fictions of Antebellum America.* Champaign: University of Illinois Press, 2002.

Heidt, Stephen. "The Presidency as Pastiche: Atomization, Circulation, and Rhetorical Instability." *Rhetoric & Public Affairs* 15 (2012): 623–33.

Heith, Diane J. "Staffing the White House Public Opinion Apparatus 1969–1988." *Public Opinion Quarterly* 62, no. 2 (1998): 165–89.

Hemmings, Clare. "Invoking Affect: Cultural Theory and the Ontological Turn." *Cultural Studies* 19 (2005): 548–67.

Hertsgaard, Mark. *On Bended Knee: The Press and the Reagan Presidency.* New York: Farrar Strauss and Giroux, 1988.

Hill, Kim Quale. "The Policy Agenda of the President and the Mass Public: A Research Validation and Extension." *American Journal of Political Science* 42 (1998): 1328–34.

Hoffman, Karen S. *Popular Leadership in the Presidency: Origins and Practices.* Lanham, MD: Lexington Books, 2010.

Hogan, Michael J. *Woodrow Wilson's Western Tour: Rhetoric, Public Opinion, and the League of Nations.* College Station: Texas A&M University Press, 2006.

Holbert, R. Lance. "A Typology for the Study of Entertainment Television and Politics." *American Behavioral Scientist* 49, number 3 (2005): 436–53.

Hult, Karen M., and Charles E. Walcott. *Empowering the White House: Governing under Nixon, Ford, and Carter.* Lawrence: University Press of Kansas, 2003.

Ivie, Robert L. "Images of Savagery in American Justifications for War." *Communications Monographs* 47, number 4 (1980): 279–94.

Ivie, Robert L., and Oscar Giner. "American Exceptionalism in a Democratic Idiom: Transacting the Mythos of Change in the 2008 Presidential Campaign." *Communication Studies* 60 (2009): 359–75.

Iyengar, Shanto, and Donald R. Kinder. *News That Matters.* Chicago: University of Chicago Press, 1987.

Iyengar, Shanto, and Adam Simon. "News Coverage of the Gulf Crisis and Public Opinion: A Study of Agenda-Setting, Priming, and Framing," *Communication Research* 20 (1993): 365–83.

Jacobs, Lawrence R. "Communicating from the White House: Presidential Narrowcasting and the National Interest." *The Executive Branch*, edited by Joel D. Auberbach and Mark A. Peterson (Oxford: Oxford University Press, 2005): 174–208.

Jacobs, Lawrence R., and Melanie Burns. "The Second Face of the Public Presidency: Presidential Polling and the Shift from Policy to Personality Polling." *Presidential Studies Quarterly* 34 (2004): 536–56.

Jamieson, Kathleen Hall. *Eloquence in an Electronic Age: The Transformation of Political Speechmaking.* New York: Oxford University Press, 1990.

Jamieson, Kathleen M. Hall. "Generic Constraints and the Rhetorical Situation." *Philosophy & Rhetoric* 6 (1973): 162–70.

Jamieson, Kathleen Hall. *Packaging the Presidency*, 3rd ed. New York: Oxford University Press, 1996.

Jamieson, Kathleen Hall, and Karlyn Kohrs Campbell. "Rhetorical Hybrids: Fusions of Generic Elements." *Quarterly Journal of Speech* 68 (1982): 146–57.

Jones, John M., and Robert C. Rowland. "The Weekly Radio Addresses of President Ronald Reagan." *Journal of Radio Studies* 7 (2000): 257–81.

Kaufman, Burton I. *The Post Presidency from Washington to Clinton.* Lawrence: University Press of Kansas, 2012.

Keith, William M., and Christian O. Lundberg. *The Essential Guide to Rhetoric.* Boston: Bedford/ St. Martin's, 2008.

Kengor, Paul. *Wreath Layer or Policy Player: The Vice President's Role in Foreign Policy.* Lanham, MD: Lexington Books, 2000.

Kernell, Samuel. *Going Public: New Strategies of Presidential Leadership.* 4th ed. Washington, DC: CQ Press, 2006.

Kiewe, Amos. *The Modern Presidency and Crisis Rhetoric.* New York: Praeger, 1994.

Kumar, Martha Joynt. "Communications Operations in the White House of President George W. Bush: Making News on His Terms." *Presidential Studies Quarterly* 33 (2003): 366–93.

Kumar, Martha Joynt. *Managing the President's Message: The White House Communications Operation.* Baltimore: Johns Hopkins University Press, 2010.

Kurr, Jeff. "The Construction of Digital Borders in Obama's Enhanced State of the Union." Paper presented at the annual meeting of the Rhetoric Society of America, May 2014.

Kuypers, Jim A. *Presidential Crisis Rhetoric and the Press in the Post-Cold War World.* New York: Greenwood Publishing Group, 1997.

Lang, Gladys Engel, and Kurt Lang. "Polling on Watergate: The Battle for Public Opinion." *Public Opinion Quarterly* 44 (1980): 530–47.

Laracey, Mel. *Presidents and the People; The Partisan Story of Going Public.* College Station, TX: Texas A&M University Press, 2010.

LeLoup, Lance, and Steven Shull, *The President and Congress: Collaboration and Combat in National Policymaking.* 2nd ed. New York: Pearson, 2002.

Lewis, William F. "Telling America's Story: Narrative Form and the Reagan Presidency." *Quarterly Journal of Speech* 73 (1987): 280–302.

Lim, Elvin T. "Five Trends in Presidential Rhetoric: An Analysis of Rhetoric from George Washington to Bill Clinton." *Presidential Studies Quarterly* 32 (2002): 228–45.

Lim, Elvin T. "The Presidency and the Media: Two Faces of Democracy." In *The Presidency and the Political System*, 10th ed., edited by Michael Nelson 258–71. Washington, DC: CQ Press, 2013.

Linsky, Martin. *Impact: How the Press Affects Federal Policymaking.* New York: WW Norton, 1986.

Lowi, Theodore J. *The Personal Presidency: Power Invested, Promise Unfulfilled.* Ithaca: Cornell University Press, 1985.

Lucas, Stephen E. "Genre Criticism and Historical Context: The Case of George Washington's First Inaugural Address." *Quarterly Journal of Speech* 41, no. 4 (1986): 354–370.

Lucas, Stephen E., and Martin J. Medhurst. "Top 100 Speeches of the Twentieth Century." http://americanrhetoric.com/newtop-100speeches.htm.

Maltese, John A. *Spin Control: The White House Office of Communications and the Management of Presidential News.* Charlotte: University of North Carolina Press, 1994.

Martin, Martha Anna. "Ideologues, Ideographs, and 'The Best Men': From Carter to Reagan." *Southern Speech Communication Journal* 49 (1983): 12–25.

Mayer, Jeremy D. "The Presidency and Image Management: Discipline in Search of Illusion." *Presidential Studies Quarterly* 34 (2004): 620–31.

McCombs, Maxwell, and Donald E. Shaw. "The Agenda Setting Function of Mass Media." *Public Opinion Quarterly* 36 (1972): 176–87.

McDonald, Ian R., and Regina G. Lawrence. "Filling the 24×7 News Hole: Television News Coverage Following September 11." *American Behavioral Scientist* 48 (2004): 327–40.

Medhurst, Martin J. "Atoms for Peace and Nuclear Hegemony: The Rhetorical Structure of a Cold War Campaign," *Armed Forces & Society* 23 (1997): 571–59.

Medhurst, Martin J., ed. *Beyond the Rhetorical Presidency.* College Station: Texas A&M University Press, 1996.

Medhurst, Martin J. *Dwight D. Eisenhower: Strategic Communicator.* Westport, CT: Greenwood Press, 1993.

Medhurst, Martin J. "Eisenhower and the Crusade for Freedom: The Rhetorical Origins of a Cold War Campaign," *Presidential Studies Quarterly* 27 (1997): 646–61.

Medhurst, Martin J. "Reconceptualizing Rhetorical History: Eisenhower's Farewell Address." *Quarterly Journal of Speech* 80 (1994): 195–218.

Medhurst, Martin J. "Religious Rhetoric and the Ethos of Democracy: A Case Study of the 2000 Presidential Campaign." *The Ethos of Rhetoric,* edited by Michael J. Hyde (University of South Carolina Press, 2004): 114–35.

Medhurst, Martin J., Robert L. Ivie, Philip Wander, and Robert L. Scott. *Cold War Rhetoric: Strategy, Metaphor, and Ideology.* East Lansing: Michigan State University Press, 2012.

Mercieca, Jennifer R. *Founding Fictions.* Tuscaloosa: University of Alabama Press, 2012.

Milkis, Sidney M. *Political Parties and Constitutional Government: Remaking American Democracy.* Baltimore: Johns Hopkins University Press, 1999.

Milkis, Sidney M. *The President and the Parties: The Transformation of the American Party System since the New Deal.* New York: Oxford University Press, 1993.

Milkis, Sidney M., and Jerome M. Mileur, eds. *The New Deal and the Triumph of Liberalism.* Amherst: University of Massachusetts Press, 2002.

Milkis, Sidney M., and Jerome M. Mileur, eds. *Progressivism and the New Democracy.* Amherst: University of Massachusetts Press, 1999.

Miroff, Bruce. "From 'Midcentury' to Fin-de-Siècle: The Exhaustion of the Presidential Image." *Rhetoric & Public Affairs* 1 (1998): 185–99.

Murphy, John M. "'Our Mission and Our Moment': George W. Bush and September 11," *Rhetoric and Public Affairs* 6 (2003): 607–32.

Nelson, Michael, and R. L. Riley. *The President's Words: Speeches and Speechmaking in the Modern White House.* Lawrence: University Press of Kansas, 2010.

Noonan, Peggy. *What I Saw at the Revolution: A Political Life in the Reagan Era.* New York: Random House, 1990.

Norrander, Barbara. "Presidential Nomination Politics in the Post-Reform Era." *Political Research Quarterly* 49 (1996): 875–915.

O'Connor, Karen, Bernadette Nye, and Laura Van Assendelft. "Wives in the White House: The Political Influence of First Ladies." *Presidential Studies Quarterly* 26 (1996): 835–53.

Osborn, Michael. "Archetypal Metaphor in Rhetoric: The Light-Dark Family." *Quarterly Journal of Speech* 53, number 2 (1967): 115–26.

Osborn, Michael. "The Evolution of the Archetypal Sea in Rhetoric and Poetic." *Quarterly Journal of Speech* 63 (1977): 347–63.

Osborn, Michael. "The Trajectory of My Work with Metaphor." *Southern Communication Journal* 74, number 1 (January–March 2009): 79–87.

Osborn, Michael, and Douglas Ehninger. "Metaphor in Public Address." *Speech Monographs* 29 (1962): 223–34.

Parenti, Michael. *Make-Believe Media: The Politics of Entertainment.* New York: St. Martin's Press, 1992.

Parry-Giles, Shawn J., and Trevor Parry-Giles. "Collective Memory, Political Nostalgia, and the Rhetorical Presidency: Bill Clinton's Commemoration of the March on Washington, August 28, 1998." *Quarterly Journal of Speech* 86 (2000): 417–37.

Parry-Giles, Shawn, and Trevor Parry-Giles. *Constructing Clinton: Hyperreality and Presidential Image-Making in Postmodern Politics.* New York: Peter Lang, 2002.

Parry-Giles, Shawn J., and Trevor Parry-Giles. "Gendered Politics and Presidential Image Construction: A Reassessment of the 'Feminine Style.'" *Communications Monographs* 63 (1996): 337–53.

Parry-Giles, Trevor, and Shawn Parry-Giles. "The *West Wing*'s Primetime Presidentiality: Mimesis and Catharsis in a Postmodern Romance." *Quarterly Journal of Speech* 88 (2002): 209–27.

Patterson, Thomas E., and Robert D. McClure. *The Unseeing Eye: The Myth of Television Power in National Elections.* New York: Putnam, 1976.

Paulson, Jon. "Theodore Roosevelt and the Rhetoric of Citizenship: On Tour in New England, 1902," *Communication Quarterly* 50 (2002): 123–34.

Peake, Jeffrey S. "Presidential Agenda Setting in Foreign Policy." *Political Research Quarterly* 54 (2002): 69–86.

Perelman, Chaim, and Lucie Olbrechts-Tyteca. *The New Rhetoric: A Treatise on Argumentation.* Notre Dame, IN: University of Notre Dame Press, 1989.

Piven, Frances Fox, and Richard Cloward, *Poor Peoples' Movements: Why They Succeed, How They Fail.* New York: Vintage, 1978.

Prelli, Lawrence J. *Rhetorics of Display.* Columbia: University of South Carolina Press, 2006.

Prior, Markus. "News vs. Entertainment: How Increasing Media Choice Widens Gaps in Political Knowledge and Turnout." *American Journal of Political Science* 49 (2005): 577–92.

Regan, Don. *For the Record: From Wall Street to Washington.* New York: Harcourt, Brace, Jovanovich, 1988.

Reinsch, J. Leonard. *Getting Elected; From Radio and Roosevelt to Television and Reagan.* 2nd ed. New York: Hippocrene, 1996.

Reyes, G. Mitchell. "The Swift Boat Veterans for Truth, the Politics of Realism, and the Manipulation of Vietnam Remembrance in the 2004 Presidential Election." *Rhetoric & Public Affairs* 9 (2006): 571–600.

Riley, Denise. *Impersonal Passion: Language as Affect.* Durham, NC: Duke University Press, 2005.

Ritter, Kurt, and Martin J. Medhurst, eds. *Presidential Speechwriting: From the New Deal to the Reagan Revolution and Beyond.* College Station: Texas A&M University Press, 2004.

Rogin, Michael. *Ronald Reagan: The Movie and Other Episodes in Political Demonology.* Berkeley: University of California Press, 1988.

Rojecki, Andrew. "Rhetorical Alchemy: American Exceptionalism and the War on Terror." *Political Communication* 25 (2008): 67–88.

Roochnik, David. *Of Art and Wisdom: Plato's Understanding of Techne.* University Park: Pennsylvania State University Press, 2007.

Rosentiel, Tom. *Strange Bedfellows: How Television and Presidential Candidates Change American Politics.* New York; Hyperion, 1992.

Rottinghaus, Brandon. *The Provisional Pulpit: Modern Presidential Leadership of Public Opinion.* College Station: Texas A&M University Press, 2010.

Rottinghaus, Brandon. "Surviving Scandal: The Institutional and Political Dynamics of National and State Executive Scandals." *PS: Political Science and Politics* 47 (2014): 131–40.

Rudalevige, Andrew. *The New Imperial Presidency: Renewing Presidential Power after Watergate.* Ann Arbor: University of Michigan Press, 2005.

Schaefer, Todd M. "Persuading the Persuaders: Presidential Speeches and Editorial Opinion." *Political Communication* 14 (1997): 97–111.

Scharrer, Erica, and Kim Bissell. "Overcoming Traditional Boundaries: The Role of Political Activity in Media Coverage of First Ladies." *Women & Politics* 21 (2000): 55–83.

Scheufele, Dietram A. "Agenda Setting, Priming and Framing Revisited: Another Look at Cognitive Effects of Political Communication." *Mass Communication and Society* 3 (2000): 297–316.

Schlesinger, Arthur M., Jr. *The Imperial Presidency.* New York: Mariner Books, 2004.

Schram, Martin. *The Great American Video Game: Presidential Politics in the Television Age.* New York: Morrow, 1987.

Seligman, Lester G., and Cary R. Covington. *The Coalitional Presidency.* Belmont, CA: Dorsey, 1989.

Shapiro, Robert Y. "Public Opinion, Elites, and Democracy." *Critical Review* 12 (1998): 501–28.

Shogan, Colleen J. *The Moral Rhetoric of American Presidents.* College Station: Texas A&M University Press, 2006.

Sigelman, Lee. "Presidential Inaugurals: The Modernization of a Genre." *Political Communication* 13 (1996): 81–92.

Simon, Dennis M., and Charles W. Ostrom. "The Impact of Televised Speeches and Foreign Travel on Presidential Approval." *Public Opinion Quarterly* 53 (1989): 58–82.

Smith, Craig Allen. "President Bush's Enthymeme of Evil: The Amalgamation of 9/11, Iraq, and Moral Values." *American Behavioral Scientist* 49 (2005): 32–47.

Smith, Craig R. *Confessions of a Presidential Speechwriter.* East Lansing: Michigan State University Press, 2014.

Smith, Ted J., and Michael J. Hogan. "Public Opinion and the Panama Canal Treaties of 1977." *Public Opinion Quarterly* 51 (1987): 5–30.

Southwell, Priscilla L. "A Backroom without the Smoke? Superdelegates and the 2008 Democratic Nomination Process." *Party Politics* 18 (2012): 267–83.

Spitzer, Robert J. *President and Congress: Executive Hegemony at the Crossroads of American Government.* New York: McGraw-Hill, 1993.

Strolovitch, Dara Z. *Affirmative Advocacy: Race, Class, and Gender in Interest Group Politics.* Chicago: University of Chicago Press, 2007.

Stuckey, Mary E. *Defining Americans: The Presidency and National Identity.* Lawrence: University Press of Kansas, 2004.

Stuckey, Mary E. *The Good Neighbor: Franklin D. Roosevelt and the Rhetoric of American Power.* East Lansing: Michigan State University Press, 2013.

Stuckey, Mary E. "Rethinking the Rhetorical Presidency and Presidential Rhetoric." *Review of Communication* 10 (2010): 38–52.

Stuckey, Mary E. *Slipping the Surly Bonds: Reagan's Challenger Address.* College Station: Texas A&M University Press, 2006.

Stuckey, Mary E. *Strategic Failures in the Modern Presidency.* Cresskill, NY: Hampton Press, 1997.

Stuckey, Mary E. *Voting Deliberately: Creating Citizens, 1936.* University Park: Pennsylvania State University Press, 2015.

Stuckey, Mary E., and Greg M. Smith. "The Presidency and Popular Culture." In *The Presidency, the Public, and the Parties*, edited by Michael Nelson, 211–21. Washington, DC: CQ Press, 2007.

Teten, Ryan L. "Evolution of the Modern Rhetorical Presidency: Presidential Presentation and Development of the State of the Union Address." *Presidential Studies Quarterly* 33 (2003): 333–46.

Thrush, Glenn, and Jonathan Martin. *The End of the Line: Romney vs. Obama: The 34 Days That Decided the Election*. New York: Random House, 2012.

Towle, Michael J. *Out of Touch: The Presidency and Public Opinion.* College Station: Texas A&M University Press, 2004.

Toye, Richard. *Rhetoric: A Very Short Introduction*. New York: Oxford University Press, 2013.

Tulis, Jeffrey K. *The Rhetorical Presidency.* Princeton: Princeton University Press, 1987.

Valenzano, Joseph M. III, and Jason A. Edwards. "Exceptionally Distinctive: President Obama's Complicated Articulation of American Exceptionalism." In *American Identity in the Age of Obama,*edited by Amilcar Antonio Bareto and Richard L. O'Bryant, 175–98. New York: Routledge, 2014.

Vatz, Richard E. "Public Opinion and Presidential Ethos." *Western Journal of Communication* 40 (1976): 196–206.

Vatz, Richard E. "The Myth of the Rhetorical Situation." *Philosophy and Rhetoric* 6 (1973): 154–61.

Vaughn, Justin S., and Lily J. Goren, eds. *Women and the White House: Gender, Popular Culture and Presidential Politics*. Lexington: University Press of Kentucky, 2012.

Vaughn Justin S., and Jose D. Villalobos. "Conceptualizing and Measuring White House Staff Influence on Presidential Rhetoric." *Presidential Studies Quarterly* 36 (2006): 681–88.

Walcott, Charles E., and Karen M. Hult. *Governing the White House: From Hoover through LBJ.* Lawrence: University Press of Kansas, 1995.

Ware, B. Lee, and Wil A. Linkugel, "They Spoke in Defense of Themselves: On the Generic Criticism of Apologia." *Quarterly Journal of Speech* 59 (1973): 273–83.

Washington, George. *George Washington's Rules of Civility & Decent Behavior in Company and Conversation*. Boston: Applewood Books, 1989.

Wattenberg, Martin. "The Changing Presidential Media Environment," *Presidential Studies Quarterly* 34 (2004): 557–72.

Wattenberg, Martin. *The Rise of Candidate-Centered Politics: Presidential Elections of the 1980s*. Cambridge, MA: Harvard University Press, 1991.

Wertheimer, Molly Meijer, ed. *Leading Ladies of the White House: Communication Strategies of Notable Twentieth-Century First Ladies.* Lanham, MD: Rowman & Littlefield, 2005.

White, Graham J. *FDR and the Press.* Chicago: University of Chicago Press, 1979.

Winfield, Betty Houchin. *FDR and the News Media.* New York: Columbia University Press, 1994.

Wood, B. Dan, and Jeffrey S. Peake. "The Dynamics of Foreign Policy Agenda Setting." *American Political Science Review* 92 (1998): 173–84.

Worthington, Ian, ed. *Persuasion: Greek Rhetoric in Action.* New York: Routledge, 2002.

Zaller, John, and Dennis Chiu. "Government's Little Helper: U.S. Press Coverage of Foreign Policy Crises, 1945–1991." *Political Communication* 13 (1996): 385–405.

Zarefsky, David. "Lyndon Johnson Redefines 'Equal Opportunity': The Beginnings of Affirmative Action." *Communication Studies* 31 (1980): 85–94.

Zarefsky, David. "Presidential Rhetoric and the Power of Definition," *Presidential Studies Quarterly* 34 (2004): 607–19.

Zarefsky, David. *President Johnson's War on Poverty: Rhetoric and History.* Tuscaloosa: University of Alabama Press, 1986.